IN BRIEF

Have you just started to play the drums? Are you thinking about buying a drum kit or cymbals? Do you want to find out more about the instruments you already own? This book will tell you all you need to know. You'll read about the role of a drummer in a band, about taking lessons and practising, about drums, cymbals, heads, sticks and hardware, about tuning and the history of the drum kit – and much more.

A good choice

Having read this book, you'll be in a position to get the best from your drums, and to make a good choice when selecting drums, cymbals, sticks and drum heads. And you'll be able to understand anything else you may want to read about these instruments, either in print or on the Internet.

Start at the beginning

If you have just started playing, or haven't yet begun, pay particular attention to the first four chapters. If you've been playing a while, you may prefer to skip ahead to Chapter 5.

Glossary

In the glossary at the end of the book you'll find short definitions of most of the terms you'll come across as a drummer. To make life even easier, the glossary doubles as an index.

CONTENTS

1. THE DRUMS

You hear some pretty wild stories about drummers: they're savages who hit everything in sight. They always play as loudly as they can. They can't read – music that is. And then there's the one about the four-piece band: three musicians and a drummer...

It's all jealousy really. Every musician knows the importance of the role of the drummer. The drummer is the engine of the band – and if your engine's not running properly, you won't get anywhere.

The drummer

So why is the drummer so important? They're the member of the band who keeps everything together, who gets everyone to start and stop at the right time, who makes sure nobody speeds up or slows down, and who reminds the singer where to come in. And it's the drummer that makes the music swing or groove. So there's a lot of truth in the saying 'a band's as good as its drummer'.

Many styles

As a drummer, you can play a wide variety of styles, from country music to jazz, grunge, soul, funk, R&B and heavy metal. You can play in bands where you need lots of amplification in order to be heard, or in groups where you need to play as softly as possible just so the audience can still hear what an unamplified pianist is doing. You can play in all sorts of different ensembles, from trios to big bands. And you can play improvised music and music that's written down note for note.

Easy to learn

One of the great things about drumming is that it's quite easy to learn. You may be able to play a basic rock beat within a couple of weeks, and within a couple of months you'll probably be able to play along to most of the songs in the charts. Ultimately, however, drums are just as hard to master as any other instrument.

Create your own

Almost every guitar has six strings. Every trumpet has three valves. Every piano looks basically the same. As a drummer, however, you can create your own instrument. You decide how many drums and how many cymbals you use, what your kit looks like and how you tune it.

Loud and soft

A drum kit is one of the loudest acoustic instruments there is, and yet you can learn how to play the drums without making too much noise. For example, you can get special practice kits, you can do all kinds of exercises on pillows – even just playing your thighs with your hands helps. There's more on this in Chapter 3.

2. A QUICK TOUR

A drum kit is a set of drums, a set of cymbals and a bunch of stands and pedals collectively known as the hardware. This chapter introduces the main elements of the basic five-piece drum kit, as used by most beginners but also some professional players.

A five-piece kit actually has at least ten separate components – the 'five' just refers to the number of actual drums. The two main drums are the high-pitched, crisp-sounding *snare drum* and the low-tuned *bass drum*. The other three are the toms: two of which are attached to the bass drum, and one of which stands on the floor.

Cymbals

Besides drums, a kit has various cymbals. The biggest is the *ride cymbal*, which is used to play a constant pattern (sometimes called the 'ride') in many rhythms. This pattern of beats can also be played on the *hi-hat cymbals*. These are a pair of cymbals, one mounted above the other, which you can play either by closing them with a spring-loaded pedal or by striking the top cymbal with a stick. For accented beats you use a thinner type of cymbal called a *crash cymbal*.

Stands and pedals

The ride and crash cymbals are mounted on cymbal stands, and there is a special type of stand for the snare drum. The two small toms are usually mounted on a tom holder, which is itself mounted on the bass drum. The bass drum is played with a foot pedal, as is the hi-hat.

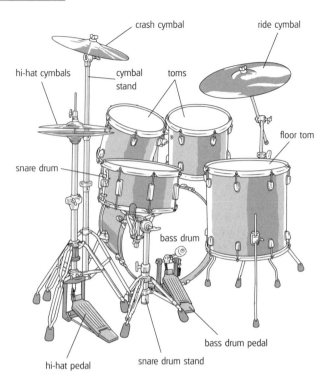

crash cymbal

ride cymbal

hi-hat cymbals

cymbal stand

toms

floor tom

snare drum

bass drum

bass drum pedal

hi-hat pedal

snare drum stand

A five-piece kit with ride, crash and hi-hat cymbals

As big as you like

You can make a drum kit as big as you like. Most drummers use additional cymbals, such as two or three crashes, and many also add extra toms, bass drums and other equipment. Chapter 15 shows some examples of drum kits, from a four-piece jazz set-up to a nine-piece rock kit.

The shell

The main part of a drum is called the *shell*. This is the *sound box* of the drum. Snare drums often have metal shells, but the other drums usually have wooden ones.

The heads

Most drums come with two heads. The *batter head* is the head you play. Underneath is the *bottom head*, which is also known as the *resonant head*. If you take this bottom head off a drum the sound becomes noticeably less resonant – the tone will be shorter and less full.

Rods, lugs and hoops

To tune a drum you tighten the tension in the head, by turning the *tension rods* into the *lugs*. This pulls down the *counter hoop*, which grips the head by its *flesh hoop*, and pulls it over the drum.

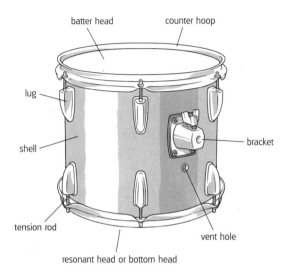

batter head   counter hoop

lug

shell   bracket

tension rod

vent hole

resonant head or bottom head

The main parts of a drum

The main drums

You can play around ninety percent of all the songs in the charts with just a bass drum, a snare drum and a pair of hi-hat cymbals. This is because in many styles the bass drum and the snare drum provide the central beat of the music, the bass drum playing every *downbeat* (one and three) and the snare drum every *upbeat* (two and four). It sounds something like *boom, crack, boom, crack...* The other drums and cymbals are basically there for embellishment – they are used to play fills, to break between two sections of a song, to spice up the basic beat and to play solos.

The bass drum

Because it's played with a pedal, the bass drum is also known as the *kick drum*. It has a low, deep, heavy and fairly short sound. Most drummers use a 22x16 bass drum – meaning the drum head size is 22" and the shell is 16" deep – though other sizes are available (see pages 37–38). *Spurs* on either side of the bass drum keep it from rolling over or creeping away from you.

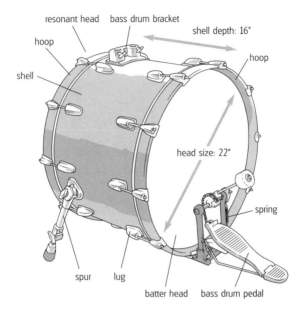

A 22x16 bass drum with bass drum pedal

The snare drum

Both the sound and the name of the snare drum come from the set of *snares* – some twenty spiralled metal strands – which are mounted against the bottom head. Every time you hit the drum the snares bounce from, and immediately snap back to, the bottom head, creating a crisp, tight sound. Most snare drums are 14" in diameter with a depth of between 5" and 6.5", though other sizes are available (see pages 35–36). The deeper the drum, the deeper the sound will be.

Snare strainer

The *snare strainer* is a catch that allows you to disengage the snares, lowering them from the bottom head, which makes the drum more like a high-pitched tom. A knurled knob on the snare strainer also lets you vary the tension on the snares, making them tighter or looser to vary the sound.

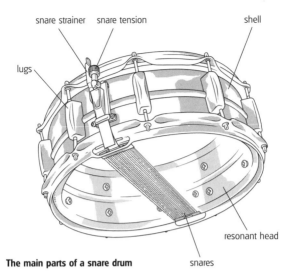

The main parts of a snare drum

snare strainer snare tension shell

lugs

resonant head

snares

Toms

The toms, or *tom-toms*, are used mainly for fills and solos. They come in a wide variety of sizes, and the bigger a drum is, the lower it can sound. A typical five-piece kit has two smaller toms, a 12" and a 13", mounted directly on the bass drum. For this reason they're also known as *rack toms*, *mounted toms* or *hanging toms*. The third tom is the *floor tom*, usually 16" in diameter. It stands on its own, to the right of the drummer.

Fusion

One of the main variations on this set-up is known as a *fusion kit*, with 10" and 12" toms, a stand-mounted 'hanging' 14" tom and a 20" or 22" bass drum.

Power toms

Rack toms come in various depths. Traditionally, a 12" tom is 8" deep (12x8), but *power toms* are usually two inches deeper (12x10). There are also in-between sizes. The deeper a tom is, the deeper its sound will be. Most floor toms have *square sizes*, such as 16x16.

Head first

Drums are usually identified by their head size only: a 12" drum is a drum with a 12" diameter head. And when both the head size and the depth are given, the head size comes first – so a 12x10 drum has a 12" head and a shell depth of 10". However, in the US, they do it the other way around. In other words, a European 12x10 equals an American 10x12. A basic rule avoids confusion: the higher number always refers to the head size.

CYMBALS

A basic cymbal set consists of a ride cymbal, a pair of hi-hats and a crash cymbal. The hi-hats are played with your (left) foot. This is done by closing them with the pedal, playing them with sticks or, most frequently, a combination of the two.

Keeping time

If you play a basic rock rhythm you'll play a constant pattern on the closed hi-hat cymbals or on the ride cymbal. This is called *keeping time*. Using the hi-hats produces a tighter, more defined sound, whilst the ride cymbal creates a more open and sustained sound.

Sizes

Most drummers go for a 20" ride, though the 22" is also quite popular. Other sizes are quite rare. The vast majority of drummers go for 14" hi-hat cymbals, whilst others prefer a 13" set.

Crashes

Crash cymbals, like toms, are named after the sound they make. And also like toms, they're mainly used for adding colour to the basic rhythm. They are thinner and smaller than ride cymbals, and respond very quickly when struck, enabling a wide array of accents. If you only have one crash cymbal, it will usually be a 16" or an 18". If you can afford two, a common choice is one of each, but many other sizes are also available.

Effect cymbals

Besides rides, crashes and hi-hats, many other cymbal types are available. These are often referred to as *effect cymbals* and range from paper-thin *splashes* to raw sounding Chinese cymbals. You can read more about these in Chapter 8.

Bow, cup and edge

The *bow* of the cymbal is where the ride is struck when played. The *cup* or *bell*, in the middle, can be used for tighter-sounding accents. Crashes are played on their edge, with a glancing motion.

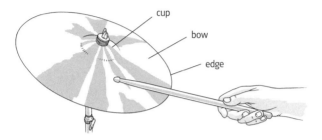

The 'parts' of a cymbal

Other components

As well as many kinds of cymbals, you can add a variety of other instruments to your kit. These range from timbales and the very popular cowbells (see page 105) to tambourines and other small percussion instruments.

STANDS AND PEDALS

Stands and pedals are collectively known as *hardware*. Most stands come with *double-braced* legs, each leg consisting of two metal strips, though lighter single-braced models are also available.

Straight and boom stands

Cymbal stands are usually made up of three telescopic tubes. The *tilter*, at the end, allows you to angle the cymbal towards you. With the extra, lateral moving arm of a *boom stand* you can basically position your cymbals anywhere you want them. There are also special boom stands on which toms can be mounted.

Snare drum stand

The snare drum is set between the three arms of the snare drum stand's *basket*. The basket is adjustable to the exact size of the drum and can also be tilted.

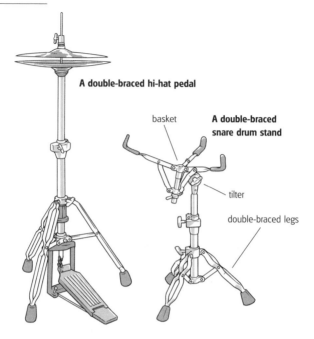

A double-braced hi-hat pedal

basket

A double-braced snare drum stand

tilter

double-braced legs

The pedals

There are a wide variety of bass drum and hi-hat pedals around. Some are very basic whilst others come with very sophisticated means of adjustment. One of the most important pedal adjustments is the *spring tension*. This allows you to make the pedal feel lighter or heavier. The spring of the bass drum pedal is shown in the illustration on page 6. The hi-hat pedal spring is usually hidden inside its lower tube.

LEFT-HANDED PLAYERS

If you're right-handed you'll probably arrange your kit something like the one illustrated at the start of this chapter. But left-handed drummers often set up the other way around, playing the bass drum with their left foot and the hi-hat with their right (see page 98). Setting up this way is not the only option for left-handed drummers – other alternatives are given in Chapter 10, *Setting Up and Maintenance*.

3. LEARNING TO PLAY

Is it hard to learn to play the drums? Do you have to take lessons, or learn to read music? And what about practising? This chapter covers all these issues, as well as tutor videos, ways to make a kit quieter, and more.

There are many good drummers, and some great ones, who are completely self-taught – they got themselves a drum kit, or perhaps just one drum, figured out a basic beat and went on from there. Yet most of the world's top drummers have consulted a teacher at one time or another, rather than trying to work everything out for themselves. Some even still do, occasionally.

What is there to learn?
Good drumming lessons are about more than just knocking out beats. They also include subjects like stick technique, posture, rudiments, dynamics, keeping time, reading music, tuning and introductions to different styles of music.

Private lessons
Though it's usually the most expensive option, taking lessons from a private teacher has certain advantages. You're likely to be taught one-to-one, and be given lots of flexibility about how often you have lessons and how long they last.

At school
Children can usually take drum lessons at school. If they are subsidized, school lessons may well work out cheaper than private lessons, though often group lessons are

provided, with two or more pupils being taught at once. Also, many schools only offer lessons on percussion, covering everything from xylophone to timpani, rather than specific drum kit lessons.

Collectives
You may also want to check whether there are any teachers' collectives or music schools in your area. These collectives may offer extras such as ensemble playing, master classes and clinics in a wide variety of styles and at various levels.

Adults
It's never too late to start learning the drums. Most adults take private lessons, but you could also consider attending an adult education class.

Small children
You can start learning to play the drums pretty well as soon as you can walk, the only problem being that a regular drum kit will be too big. There are special – and usually very affordable – junior kits available which are good enough to start out on. A regular drum kit with a smaller (18") bass drum can also be used. Unfortunately, bass drums this size are not very common in the lower price ranges.

Locating a teacher
If you're looking for a private teacher, there are various places you could try. Music shops often have teachers on staff, or they can refer you to someone. You can also consult your local Musician's Union, or a music teacher at school or college in your vicinity. You could also check the classified ads in newspapers, music magazines and on supermarket bulletin boards, or consult the *Yellow Pages*.

What will it cost?
Professional private teachers will usually charge £15–30 per hour. Some will make house-calls, for which you may pay a little extra.

Questions, questions
When enquiring about a teacher, don't simply ask how much it costs. Here are a few other questions worth asking:
• Is a free **introductory lesson** included? This will allow

you to see whether it clicks between you and the teacher
– or, for that matter, between you and the drums.

- Is the teacher still interested in taking you on if you are just playing the drums **for the fun of it**, or are you supposed to practise for hours every day?
- Are you expected to make a large investment in teaching books, or are **course materials provided**?
- Can you **record your lessons**, so that you can listen to how you sounded when you get home?
- Is this teacher going to make you **practise rudiments and technique** for ages, or will they focus more on playing with a band?

READING MUSIC

Have you ever seen a drummer reading music on stage?
Probably not. Yet many of them can read music, and it's
not hard to learn - the theory book in this series, *The
Rough Guide to Reading Music & Basic Theory*, teaches you
the basics in a few chapters.

Five lines

Drum music is written on the same stave as music for
other instruments. The main difference, however, is that
the position of the notes on the lines does not indicate a
certain pitch, but a certain part of the drum kit: every part
of the kit has its own position on, or between, the five
lines. Another difference is that the cymbals are indicated
by crosses instead of round note-heads. Here's how a basic
rock rhythm looks.

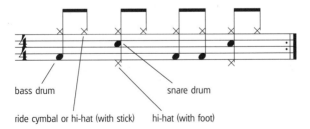

bass drum

snare drum

ride cymbal or hi-hat (with stick)   hi-hat (with foot)

A basic rock rhythm

Why read?

Is there any point in learning to read music if you're a

drummer? Certainly you can manage without this skill, but being able to read music has lots of advantages:

- You can benefit from the **thousands of books** that are available, from those which focus on exercises, grooves, fills or solos, to others in which famous drummers show you some tips of the trade. Drum magazines also often have pages of written-down material.
- If you can read music, **you can also write it**. If you hear or figure out a good beat or fill, writing it down is easier and more reliable than remembering it.
- You'll be able to **turn up and play** with any band or group that uses sheet music.
- You'll understand more **musical terms** – you won't be lost, for example, if somebody asks you to play sixteenths instead of eighths.

PRACTISING

Many top drummers practise for many hours every day, but you should be able to make decent progress with just half an hour per day. The more often you practise, the faster you'll learn, though as with any other instrument, you're better off practising half an hour a day than a couple of hours once a week.

Less noise

Drums make a great deal of noise, but you don't have to annoy your family, neighbours or flatmates every time you want to practise. Lots of musicians keep everyone happy simply by agreeing to fixed practice times, but there are also various solutions to reduce the amount of sound you make: reduce the volume of your kit; replace your drums with something less noisy; or prevent the noise from getting out. And if all else fails, you could consider doing your practice somewhere else.

Muffling your instrument

Stuffing your drums full of rags or cushions will quieten them down. However, it takes a while each time you want to turn it back into a normal kit again. What's more, even when it's stuffed completely full, the bass drum is still bound to transmit a fair amount of sound through floors and walls.

Discs and bands

A much more flexible solution is to put a series of special discs, made of rubbery materials of various hardnesses, on your drums. There are similar designs for bass drums and cymbals as well. A drawback of these discs is that they alter the way your instrument feels – the rebound of your sticks will be strongly reduced. Your cymbals will retain their feel better if you muffle them with a wide elastic band. Special bands are available for most cymbal sizes.

Gauze heads

You could also opt to replace your regular drum heads with so-called *muffling heads* or *trigger heads*, which feature a very strong type of gauze instead of the usual plastic film. These noiseless 'gauze heads' or mesh heads, which are also used on some types of electronic drums, offer a rebound that is quite similar to that of a regular head.

cymbal

cymbal pad

beater
hits rubber
pad

A practice kit

Pillows and pads

Unlike other musicians, drummers have a wide choice of alternatives for their 'real' instrument. Playing pillows, for one, has proven to be very effective for many drummers, though there are many teachers who thoroughly dislike the idea. Slightly noisier, but less dusty, are *practice pads*, which can be purchased individually or as a whole kit as shown on the previous page. Practice pads come in two basic varieties. Some have a ply of soft or hard rubber that you play on, and others have a tunable drum head with foam rubber underside.

Fast rebound

Practice discs and pads are great for reducing noise – you'll only really hear the sound of your stick hitting the surface – but most of them have a much faster rebound than real drums, so when you switch back to real drums, they tend to feel slower. Gauze heads feel more like real drum heads.

Electronic drums

Practice pads don't sound like drums, but electronic drums do. Electronic drum kits usually consist of a series of pads or shallow drums that have gauze heads with built-in *triggers*. These triggers convert your playing to electronic signals which are fed to a *sound module*, programmed with digital drum sounds. The end result can be very close (or even very, very close) to the real thing. Electronic drums are used a lot in recording studios. Their drawback is that they're still pretty expensive, starting at about a £1000, excluding amps and speakers. However, fully soundproofing a room costs a lot more.

Soundproofing

Practising on a muffled instrument or on pads allows you to work on technique and timing, but it hardly helps you develop your sound. If you want to practise on the same instrument you play on stage, soundproofing a room is an option. The costs vary greatly, depending on how much you want or need to reduce the sound. Making a room fully soundproof can cost many thousands of pounds, but less perfect solutions are much cheaper. Some people get a specialist in to do the work for them, but soundproofing is not impossible to do yourself – there are special books available on the subject.

Prefab cubicles

As an alternative to soundproofing a whole room, you could get yourself a prefab sound-reducing cubicle, which are available in a variety of makes and sizes. A decent cubicle is just as expensive as soundproofing a room to the same effect, but you can take it with you if you move, or sell it if you no longer need it.

Practising elsewhere

In most large towns and cities there are practice rooms that you can rent for one or more hours – either for a whole band or just for you. Many practice rooms come with a drum kit, often complete with a set of cymbals, so if you're lucky, all you'll need to bring with you are your sticks. Hire costs are usually quite reasonable, but to keep them to a minimum you could consider renting a room once a week and using a practice kit for the rest of the week.

PROTECTING YOUR EARS

Drumming can be harmful to your ears – even practising as little as fifteen minutes a day may cause permanent damage. And because hearing loss or damage (such as *tinnitus*, a permanent ringing sound) is usually noticed only when it's too late, prevention is the key.

Earplugs

The cheapest foam plastic earplugs, available from most music and hardware shops, will reduce the volume you

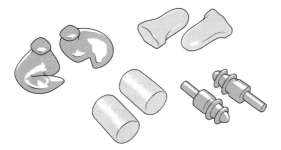

Some affordable types of ear plugs

hear greatly, but they can also make the band you're playing with sound as if they're in a different room. The most expensive earplugs, which are custom-made to fit your ears, have adjustable filters, which reduce the volume but hardly affect the sound. These aren't cheap, but a hearing aid will cost more in the long run. If you don't like sticking things in your ear, you could try using ear muffs, though you may look a little stupid.

DRUM MACHINES, VIDEOS AND MORE

You can buy all kinds of things to make practising more effective and fun.

Keeping time

Drummers are supposed to keep a band from speeding up or slowing down. To some drummers this comes very easily – they have a natural sense of tempo that keeps them steady at every speed. Most drummers don't, however, and that's where metronomes come in. These small electronic or mechanical (wind-up) devices click or bleep in a steady tempo that you set yourself.

Loud?

A metronome doesn't have to be really loud in order to be heard. As soon as you fall a bit out, your hit will not coincide with the metronome's beat. You'll hear it, and that'll tell you you're out. However, it's worth going for one that is reasonably loud, and ideally has an adjustable volume level. Most electronic metronomes also have an LED that blinks to indicate the beat; this is also useful.

Drum machines

There are also special metronomes for drummers, each with a variety of built-in sounds, and even programming facilities, which allow you to store the tempos of a number of songs. These metronomes can also play at higher volume levels, and often have headphone sockets. There are also modules available with other features, such as the option to program a bass pattern to play along to. Another device is the *phrase trainer*, which can be used to slow down a musical phrase from a CD, for example, enabling you to figure out even the meanest, fastest fills and rhythms at your own tempo. You can also do this with the right computer software.

A special programmable drummer's metronome, with extra volume and sounds (Tama)

Videos and CDs

As well as drum books, there are a great deal of tutor videos and CDs available, designed to help your practice. Most of them are made by well-known drummers who take you through loads of skills, tips and tricks. They usually last between thirty and ninety minutes, and sometimes come with a book or some sheet music of the rhythms and exercises demonstrated.

Playing along

Regular CDs are also great for practising. Put on your favourite band, grab a pair of headphones, get behind your kit and off you go. Thousands of drummers have learnt a great deal this way. Practising rudiments, either on a real drum or on something less noisy can be a lot more fun if you do it to music.

Record yourself

It's hard to really listen to yourself whilst you're playing. For this reason many musicians record their practice sessions. A stereo with a built-in microphone is all you need, though you'll get more enjoyable and useful recordings if you use better equipment, such as a MiniDisk or a decent tape recorder with a separate microphone.

And finally...

There are two great ways to learn how to play the drums, which are ultimately more important than any others. First, go and see other musicians at work; living legends or local amateurs, every gig is a learning experience. Second, play as much as you can.

4. BUYING DRUMS

You can get yourself a new five-piece drum kit with cymbals and a stool for around five or six hundred pounds. If you don't have that much to spend, you could consider buying secondhand or getting a snare drum or practice pad and building up your kit gradually. This chapter tells you what you should know before you go out shopping for drums. What to look for once you're actually in the shop is covered in Chapters 5 to 8.

A brand new five-piece drum kit can cost anywhere between about £400 and £4000, or even more. A decent kit with a decent set of cymbals, good enough to be played at proper gigs, will set you back somewhere between £800 and £1500. From that point on, things can only get better, but the differences are harder to spot.

Comparing prices

When comparing drum kit prices, take a good look at what you're going to get for your money. The cheapest kits often come with cymbals, but most are offered without. Conversely, the more you pay, the less chance there is that hardware will be included. Drum kits without hardware are usually referred to as *shell kits*, and some don't even come with a snare drum.

Hardware

If hardware does come with a kit, it will usually include bass drum and hi-hat pedals, a snare stand and a straight cymbal stand. Sometimes a second stand – perhaps a boom stand – and a stool are also included. If you plan to buy a kit that doesn't come with hardware, you could consider purchasing a pre-packed hardware set; prices start at around £200.

Better

The differences between decent starter kits and top-of-the-range professional equipment have become harder and harder to spot in recent years. So why spend the extra money?

A richer sound

A more expensive kit should produce a 'more expensive' sound – a richer sound, you might say. It should have punchier lows and brighter highs, and more colour and carrying power. The features that come with a higher price are select woods for the shells, better workmanship, more research and development into the product, original designs (rather than copies), and hardware that's sturdier, easier to adjust and better looking.

More to choose from

Paying more also usually means there are more colours and drum sizes to choose from. Low-budget series are often only available in two or three colours (usually red, white and black), and in the basic five-piece set-up – so you can't add matching toms later on.

The heads

One way in which manufacturers keep the price of entry-level kits to a minimum is to use inexpensive, low-quality heads. These stop the drums from sounding as good as they could, but fortunately it doesn't cost too much to replace them with a set of good, professional batter heads (see Chapter 7).

CYMBALS

You can get yourself a ride, a crash and a pair of hi-hat cymbals for less than £100 – but don't expect them to sound particularly good. If you want professional cymbals, be prepared to pay ten times that amount. A set of intermediate cymbals, good enough for proper gigging, will generally set you back around £400.

Nothing you can do

There's a vital difference between drums and cymbals. With good heads and tuning almost any drum kit can be made to sound at least half-decent. However, if a cheap cymbal sounds cheap, there's nothing you can do.

Cymbals first

Most people shop for drums first and then see how much they have left over for cymbals. But this can be a bad idea, as low-budget cymbals sound worse than low-budget drums ever will, so consider purchasing cymbals first.

HEADS AND STICKS

How often you have to change heads (and how long it takes to break a stick) depends largely on how hard you play, but also on the sound you're after. If you like the crisp sound of a new snare drum batter head, then you'll have to replace it long before it has worn out.

An hour or a year

There are some heavy-hitting professional drummers who replace the batter heads of their snare drums every night, and the batter heads of their toms every third night. There are also pros who use the same batter heads for over a year. As for sticks, some drummers – and definitely not just pros – go through three pairs a night, whilst others use the same pair for months.

In-between

If you play six to eight hours a week at a moderate volume the batter heads on your toms and bass drum may last six months or more before they start losing their sound. Snare drum batters go more quickly, often after one or two months. Resonant heads can stay on much longer. If you're not an aggressive drummer, a pair of sticks will last you at least a month, unless you keep time on the edge of your hi-hats.

Prices

A pair of pro-quality sticks generally costs between £7–10. A professional 14" drum head will set you back about £10–15, and most 22" heads sell for around £20–40.

SECONDHAND

For a used drum, cymbal or piece of hardware in mint condition you should expect to pay a bit over half what it would cost new. But secondhand isn't always cheaper when it comes to musical instruments – indeed, sought-after vintage equipment can sell for more than comparable new products.

Cymbals

You'll come across plenty of secondhand ride cymbals and hi-hats, whereas crashes and other cymbals are quite rare. This is because rides and hi-hats hardly ever crack, unlike thinner cymbals such as crashes and splashes. Also, drummers tend to want to replace their rides and hi-hats sooner than their crashes.

Privately or from a shop?

Used drums and cymbals can be found not only in music shops, but also in pawn shops, advertised in newspapers and music journals, on notice boards in music schools and shops, and on the Internet. Generally, purchasing a used instrument from an individual is cheaper than buying the same instrument in a music shop.

Questions

Buying a used instrument in a shop, though, does have certain advantages – mainly that you can take it back if something doesn't work properly, or if you have any questions. Another difference is that good shops rarely ask outrageous prices, but private sellers sometimes do – either because they don't know any better, or because they think you don't.

WHAT ELSE?

Here are a few more things to bear in mind when shopping for drums, cymbals and other equipment.

Sounds good, feels good

It doesn't hurt to read everything you can before going out to buy equipment. That said, if you go into a music shop, fall in love with the first kit or instrument you see, feel that it suits your playing and buy it straight off, you might end up with just as good a product. The instrument you buy should suit you in terms of sound and feel – in the end that counts more than any technical details.

Guideline

Most well-known drummers have one or more endorsements: they play instruments of a certain brand, and that company uses their name in its advertising. Such associations can be a good guideline if you're looking for a particular sound, but don't be tempted into thinking that buying the instrument of your favourite drummer will actually make you sound like them.

The music shop

A shop with an enormous number of kits on display may be slightly overwhelming, but ultimately will offer you more choice. But if there are various shops in your area, don't just go to the biggest – checking out all the retailers will allow you both to compare prices and to get the advice of different salespeople.

Try it out

In a good shop you'll be allowed to play the kits you're interested in. Some shops even have soundproofed rooms, where you can experiment in private.

Another drummer

It's always a good idea to shop with another drummer; after all, two people can see and hear more than one. This is especially true when it comes to looking at secondhand drums, as an experienced player will help you avoid passing up an excellent instrument just because it needs some repair work or a lesser-known brand with very strong attributes. Besides, it's easier to judge the sound of an instrument if someone else plays it whilst you listen from a distance.

Buying online

You can also buy musical instruments online or by mail-order. This makes it impossible to try and compare instruments, though most companies offer a return service for most or all of their products. Of course the instrument should be in perfect condition when you return it.

Catalogues, magazines and Internet

If you want to know all there is to know, then read every instrument review you can find in drummers' and musicians' magazines. Also, stock up with brochures and catalogues. A word of warning, though: besides having a wealth of information to offer, literature from manufacturers is designed to make you spend more than you have, or have in mind. The Internet is also a good source for product information. You can find more about these resources on pages 130–131.

Fairs and conventions

If a music trade fair or convention is being held in your area, check it out. Besides finding a considerable number of instruments that you can try out and compare, you will meet plenty of product specialists. Added to this you will find numerous fellow drummers, who are always a source of information and inspiration.

5. GOOD DRUMS

What a drum sounds like depends on many things, ranging from the shell's material, diameter, depth and thickness to the hoops and lugs. This chapter tells you what to look out for when buying either a single drum or a whole kit. Hardware is covered in Chapter 6, heads and sticks in Chapter 7, and cymbals in Chapter 8.

The shell is the core component of any drum. The material, its dimensions and the way it has been worked have a major effect on the sound. That's where this chapter starts, followed by some basic information on different types of lugs and hoops. Specific things to look for in snare drums, bass drums and toms follow from page 35.

Maple and birch

Many snare drums and most bass drums and toms have wooden shells. For professional drums maple is the most popular type of wood, followed by birch.

Blindfold tests

Some drummers say maple sounds warmer, some say birch does. Some find birch more percussive. Others will tell you the same about maple. Characteristics such as a wide tuning range have been ascribed to both types of wood as well. Many experts agree that maple makes for a mellower sound and a longer sustain than birch, yet others stress its 'explosive nature'. Some brands promote birch drums as 'recording drums' but many recording artists use birch drums on stage too. Even more drummers play maple both live and in the studio. And yes, most drummers fail in blindfold tests when trying to tell whether it's a maple or a birch drum kit they're listening to. The moral of this story is to go for the sound, not the wood.

Harder and brighter
Other types of wood used for drums include eucalyptus, mahogany and other hardwoods. Generally speaking, a harder wood makes for a brighter, more focused and more articulate tone.

Not specified
The type of wood used to make budget drums is often not specified. As they are made of softer woods like Filipino mahogany, basswood or lauan, these drums will usually produce a sound that can be characterized as warm, fat or round.

Outer and inner plies
Lower mid-range drums may come with one or two plies of maple or birch. An outer ply does more for the looks than the sound. A hard inner ply, though, can enhance projection, brightness and definition, and thus improve the sound.

Metal and other materials
Metal shells are used most often for snare drums. The Remo company is the inventor and sole user of Acousticon, a wood-fibre material of variable hardness, which is used for drum shells as well as for other percussion instruments. Some companies use other materials, such as carbon fibre or Plexiglas. Being hard, they generally give a louder, brighter sound.

Shell dimensions
The two main shell dimensions are diameter and depth. The wider a drum is, the lower it can be tuned. The deeper it is, the deeper its sound will be. A 12x10 tom sounds deeper than a tom in the traditional, standard size of 12x8. Today, most drum kits come with these deeper toms, usually known as *power toms*.

Thinner and thicker
Most professional drums have relatively thin shells, which

measure around 3/16"–4/16" (4.5–6.5mm). It takes good wood and craftsmanship to build shells this thin, which is one of the reasons why most lower-range drums have thicker shells, often in the 5/16"–6/16" range (8–9.5mm). Thinner drums tend to speak more easily and produce a more open, transparent sound, while thicker drums sound more focused and tight.

Plies

Shells are often made up of six or nine thin plies of wood. For mid- and higher-range shells, the exact number of plies is usually specified. A little theory: adding extra plies, and so making a shell thicker, stresses the high frequencies in the sound whilst reducing some bottom end. Having more plies, in a shell of the same thickness, makes the sound a touch drier, or tighter and less responsive. Conversely, a *solid shell*, consisting of a single ply only, makes for a very responsive drum.

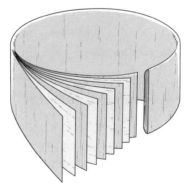

Drum shells are often made of six or nine plies

Alternative shell construction

A few small companies (Brady, Tamburo, Le Soprano, Troyan) use staves to build shells in a fashion similar to the construction of wooden congas or casks. Usually, but not always, such shells are considerably thicker than plywood shells.

The bearing edges

The *bearing edges* of a drum 'bear' the heads. Their exact shape – they are generally angled at 45 degrees – has a noticeable influence on the sound. A sharper edge makes for a sharper, brighter sound, whilst a rounder edge creates a rounder, mellower and less articulate sound. Sharp edges are only found on more expensive drums, not least because it takes longer to make them. No matter what shape they are, bearing edges should always be level and even.

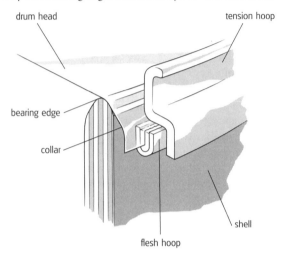

drum head   tension hoop

bearing edge

collar

shell

flesh hoop

The bearing edge 'bears' the head

Reinforcement hoops

Some drums have two extra wooden rings on their inside, close to the bearing edges. Before the development of modern production techniques they acted as reinforcement rings to keep the shell from losing its round shape. Nowadays these rings, with a width of about 1" (2.5cm), are largely used to affect the sound, and are often given

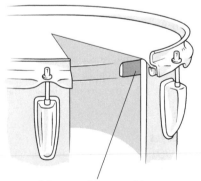

reinforcement ring or sound ring

names like *sound rings* or *sound focus rings*. That they increase the shell's thickness at its edges is supposed to slightly stress the drum's attack and higher frequencies.

Covered drums
Most lower-priced drums come with a plastic covering, which withstands scratches, bumps and most other minor knocks. This covering serves its purpose a lot better than lacquer. Check to see that the covering fits nice and snug all around the shell – the seam should ideally be held under one pair of lugs.

Lacquer and wax
Non-covered drums are usually finished with high-gloss lacquers, either solid or transparent. As an alternative they may be stained, or – occasionally – treated with wax or oil, which gives the shells a mat look. The finish on more expensive drums generally consists of a larger number of coats, making the drum look better and last longer.

ROUND AND LEVEL
The effect that the shell has on the sound of a drum is largely to do with how freely it allows the heads to vibrate – and shells that are perfectly round and level do this the best. Drums with uneven shells not only have a less perfect sound but can also be hard (or even impossible) to tune. Also, drum shells should be slightly undersized. The following checks are useful, especially when looking at older kits.

Undersized
Almost all shells are slightly narrower than the indicated size of the head. This 'floating head design' allows the head to vibrate freely. Look at the shell from the side and see if there's a small, even gap between the shell and the flesh hoop of the head. If there's no such gap the drum's sound may be restricted. It's mainly low-budget covered drums that suffer from this problem, though pro-quality drums from the 1950s–1970s can also have tight-fitting heads.

Round
If the width of the gap between the shell and the flesh hoop varies, then either the shell or the flesh hoop isn't as

round as it should be. Try replacing the head. Measuring the shell diameter at opposing lugs may show that the drum is not perfectly round – but it's hard to judge this well without some experience and good tools.

Bearing edge

Remove the heads and take a close look at the bearing edges. Trace them lightly with a fingertip. If they aren't perfectly even you may get buzzing sounds when playing the drum. A bit of very careful sanding may help, for instance if the unevenness turns out to be nothing more than a bit of spilled lacquer. Avoid drums with dented edges.

Level

To see if a shell is level you need a perfectly level surface like a sheet of plate glass (most tabletops won't do). Take the heads off, put the shell on the surface, insert a light and check to see if there's light shining from under the edge. If you don't trust the flatness of the surface, slowly rotate the drum and see what happens in various positions.

HOOPS AND LUGS

Even hoops and lugs contribute to a drum's sound, and both are available in various different designs.

Pressed hoops

The majority of drums come with *pressed hoops*, which are made of steel. However, there are various slightly heavier,

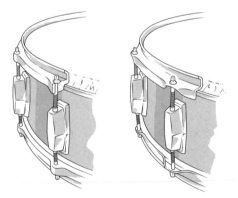

Die-cast hoop (left) and pressed hoops look very different

pressed hoops available (usually around 3/16" or 2.3mm thick), with names such as Mighty Hoops, Power Hoops and Super Hoops. They are designed to add something to the attack and make the sound a bit 'heavier' and drier. Also, their increased thickness helps to prevent warping.

Die-cast hoops

Die-cast hoops don't warp at all. You mainly find these very heavy hoops on more expensive snare drums which is where they're considered to be most effective. They add extra solidity, weight and definition to rim shots and stick shots. Some companies have die-cast hoops on their toms, but often only in the more expensive series.

Wood

Many bass drums have wooden hoops, though less expensive ones often come with synthetic or metal hoops (see page 39). Wooden hoops are also found on some expensive snare drums, and there are a few kits available that even have wooden hoops on the toms. On these drums, wooden hoops help produce a very warm, 'woody' sound.

Lugs

Lugs come in all kinds of shapes and sizes, and drums can often be recognized by their lugs. Most new drums have small lugs, known as *single lugs*. In this arrangement there's one row of lugs for each head, each lug receiving a single tension bolt. Up until the mid-1990s, though, many drums had *long lugs* or *double lugs*, which receive a tension bolt at either end. These lugs are also known as *flush bracing* or *high-tension lugs* – though the very moderate ten-

Drums with tube lugs, long lugs and small lugs

33

sion on the average drum head does not really justify the latter name.

Fashion and taste

The choice between single and double lugs depends on fashion and taste more than anything else. The same goes for variations such as the tiny *low-mass lug* or the 'classic' *tube lug*, the latter being no more than a tube with threaded ends. Some companies make all their series, from entry-level to top-of-the-range, look similar by using the same lugs on each; other companies do the opposite, giving every series a unique look.

Self-aligning

The *self-aligning nuts* in most lugs help prevent you from damaging the thread of both nuts and tension rods, and they also allow for slightly different hoop sizes. These nuts are kept in place by plastic inserts, which sometimes double as anti-detune devices by exerting a slight pressure on the tension rods.

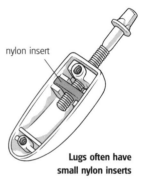

nylon insert

Lugs often have small nylon inserts

How many?

Most 22" bass drums and 14" snares have ten lugs for each head. Toms up to 13" usually have six and larger toms come with eight. Cheaper kits may have fewer lugs, which doesn't affect the ease of tuning or the tuning stability as much as you might think.

A coarser sound

Some high-end snare drums only have eight lugs per head, not to cut costs but to produce a sound that could be described as more coarse and open. And some brands use just five lugs on 10" toms – this doesn't harm the sound or the tuning stability, but it may take some getting used to when tuning.

Gaskets

Small gaskets underneath the lugs are sometimes advertised

as sound-enhancing items. Their main task, however, is to prevent the lugs from damaging the wooden exterior of the shell. Most covered drums come without such gaskets.

Plating and coating
Traditionally, all hardware is chrome-plated, as chrome is more durable and less susceptible to scratching than any other finish. However, gold-plated and solid brass hardware is also available.

THE SNARE DRUM
Snare drums are the most personal part of a kit. Professional touring drummers who don't bring their own kits with them still often take their own snare drums. Also, many drummers have more than one snare drum so they can pick a specific sound for a particular style or mood. A shallow snare with a tight sound suits funky stuff, for example, whilst a deep one is ideal for heavy backbeats.

Replacing the snare
In an entry-level kit, the snare is most often the one drum that doesn't match the quality of the rest of the kit. Drummers often replace their first snare with a better one as soon as their budget permits.

Material
Snare drums come in a wide variety of shell materials, both wood and metal. Wooden shells tend to produce quite a warm and fat sound, whilst metal shells sound brighter and project sound better. Most metal snares have steel shells, but brass and bronze models are also available, and generally said to produce a slightly mellower tone.

Snare sizes
The best-selling snare drum sizes range from 14x5 to 14x6.5. The deeper the shell, the deeper the sound. For a really meaty, beefy sound you could try a 14x8, though drums this size are quite rare. Smaller, high-pitched snares are mainly used as add-ons, often positioned to the left of the hi-hat. *Piccolos* are most popular for that purpose, ranging in size from 13x3 up to 14x4. Smaller snare drums, with 12" or 10" heads, come with non-standardized names

like *soprano* and *sopranino*. Again, depth is a major factor. A 12x7 drum, for example, will produce a deep-toned yet high-pitched sound.

14x8 and 14x3.5 snare drums

Snare strainers

Most snare strainers are quite straightforward *throw-off* affairs, and that's basically all you need. They shouldn't rattle in the 'off' position and are supposed to be operable quietly and easily, without any need to support the drum with your other hand.

Tension

Good snare strainers also allow you to adjust the snare tension. If so, adjust the tension while tapping the head so you can hear what's going on. Knobs on both the strainer and the butt end make it easier to centre the snares. There's more on this in Chapter 9, *Tuning and muffling*.

Strings and straps

The actual snares are attached to the strainer system with either strings or straps. Strings are more likely to break than straps, but both can last for years. When trying out snare drums always check that the snares are centred, with either end an equal distance from the edge. To find out whether the tension is same in all the snares, very gently compare the tightness of the outer strands. Be careful, though – if you accidentally over-stretch a strand, it will rattle until you cut it off.

Snare bed

For a non-buzzing, tight and crisp sound the snares should touch the bottom head over their entire length. Snare drum shells have been modelled for this purpose – when looking along the snares you'll see that the shell is a bit shallower where the strings or straps run over the edges. Because of this so-called *snare bed* the snare-side head-surface is slightly concave, allowing for optimal head-to-snare contact.

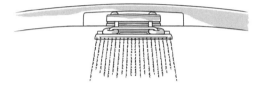

The snare bed: the shell is a little shallower where the strings or straps run over the edges

Over the edge

Parallel action strainers are quite complicated snare systems that keep the snares under tension whilst in the 'off' position. Along with the similar but simpler *semi-parallel* systems, they have long snares that extend over the edges of the drum. These systems were once popular – the extended snares were said to have a better response – but both versions have basically disappeared today, and they're only found on a few high-end snare drums.

THE BASS DRUM

The bigger the drum, the lower it will sound, and the longer it will sound for. For bass drums low is OK, but long isn't. That's why most bass drums are muffled, making for a rather short, punchy and solid sound. There are exceptions though – many jazz drummers, for example, go for a more sustained and open sounding bass drum.

Sizes

The 22x16 bass drum has been the most popular size for many years, mainly thanks to its versatility. The size is good for use in many different situations, giving plenty of bottom end without losing focus or definition. Previously, though, the best-selling bass drum size was the 22x14. Jazz drummers traditionally go for a much smaller bass drum (18x14 or 18x16) with quite a high tuning.

In-between, or bigger
Bass drum shell depths usually vary from 14" (still known as 'standard depth') to 18" and sometimes more, with extra inches adding depth to the sound. The 20" bass drum, which produces more low end than an 18" and more focus than a 22", gained popularity when fusion took off. If you like lots of low end you may want to try a 24" or even the rare 26".

Kits for kids
A kit with an 18" or even a 16" bass drum can be appropriate for a young player. However, 18" bass drums are hard to find in the lower price ranges. There are special drum kits for kids, but they're usually of a lesser quality than the average entry-level full-size option.

Tension rods
In the past, bass drums were always tuned using T-rods but by the late 1990s most of these had been replaced by standard key rods. These allow smaller, tighter-fitting cases and give the drum a neater look – after all, it's impossible to precisely tune your bass drum heads and keep the T-handles in line with the bass drum hoop.

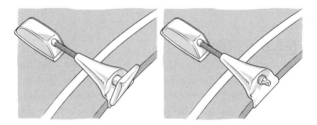

A traditional T-rod and a standard key rod on a bass drum hoop

Fast adjustment
A plus point for T-rods is that they do allow for fast adjustment of the bass drum sound. You may want to do this quite often, as getting a good bass drum sound tends to be more dependent on room acoustics than with the

other drums. Often just a few turns on one or two T-rods on the batter side are enough to give a bass drum a fat, dry sound for some songs or a higher, more resonant tuning for others.

Hoops

Most entry-level kits come with hollow metal bass drum hoops with a small rubber insert to allow proper attachment of the bass drum pedal. Wooden hoops, as found in higher price ranges, add a bit of warmth to the sound of the drum. Mid-range drums are often fitted with hoops that are made of synthetic materials such as ABS. They may not look as good as wood, but they're more durable and don't really sound that different.

Claw hooks

Wooden hoops are easily damaged, not only by being banged against things, but also by the *claw hooks* that hold them in place. These rarely fit the profile of a hoop exactly and can easily dig into the wood. For this reason, when replacing bass drum heads, always put the hoops back in their original position so the claws don't make unnecessary marks. Some high-end kits feature die-cast claw hooks instead of standard pressed ones, and occasionally kits come with felt inlays in the hooks. Plastic hoops don't use claw hooks at all – they have built-in 'ears', just like tom and snare drum hoops.

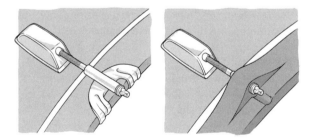

A wooden hoop with claw hooks and a plastic one with 'ears'

Spurs

Though some spurs may look very impressive they don't do much more than prevent the bass drum from rolling over or sliding away from you. Most designs offer one preset angle, which is basically all you need. Setting the height of the spurs is something you'll probably do just once.

Spikes

Spurs come with sharp spikes for use on wood or carpets. For other surfaces (and if you want to avoid bleeding shins and other damage during transportation), you can replace these spikes with rubber tips. Usually this is a matter of twisting the rubber tips up along the threaded end of the spurs. Bayonet catches work even better for this purpose, but they're rare. Less rare, unfortunately, are the designs that require you to pull the rubber tip off with your fingernails. Some floor tom legs come with convertible feet too.

Toms on a rack

On some higher-end kits the rack toms are mounted on separate stands or on a *drum rack*, rather than on the bass drum. This is partially because the bass drum sound is believed to be enhanced by relieving it of the weight of the toms – a point open to debate as the bass drum is usually muffled anyway. More importantly, many high-end bass drums have very thin shells which are not designed to carry the weight of two toms and a holder. There's more about drum racks on pages 58–59.

TOMS

Rack toms and floor toms are available in an incredibly wide variety of sizes, some series even featuring a choice of three or more shell depths for each diameter.

Rack toms

The most extended drum series offer rack toms from 8" up to 16", in even numbers but including 13" and 15". Occasionally, 6" toms are available too.

12" and 13"

The 'standard' kit, as it has been sold for many years, comes with 12" and 13" rack toms, which are quite close in size and therefore pitch as well. The 16" floor tom that comes with this standard set-up is substantially bigger and lower. If you want even differences in pitch between your three toms, this isn't ideal (see page 81).

Fusion and other sizes

As an alternative, many brands offer so-called fusion kits. These have smaller toms, with head sizes two inches apart. Such a kit, often consisting of 10", 12" and 14" toms, is much easier to tune to even intervals. In many series, though not the budget ones, you can choose your own sizes.

A different sound

When selecting sizes, pitch is not the only consideration. For example, in a traditional jazz set-up, the first tom, a 12", may be tuned considerably higher than a 10" tom from a rock drum kit. And apart from a higher pitch, it will have a different sound, even if both drums are from the same brand and series. The 12" will produce a tighter sound with lots of attack, while the 10" will sound fatter and bigger than it really is.

Five options

There may be a number of shell depths to choose from, depending on the brand and model of the drum. Most pro and semipro series offer two choices, whilst entry-level series usually offer just one, but some brands offer as many as five options. Taking a 12" tom as an example, these might be:

- The description **power toms** generally refers to two variations, 12x11 and, more commonly, 12x10. These have been the most popular sizes for years.
- The traditional **standard size**, 12x8, is mainly used in jazz and fusion.
- An **in-between size**, 12x9, started to gain popularity in the late 1990s. Though usually marketed under names that suggest a fast response, a traditional 12x8 will always be even faster. Kits featuring these in-between sizes usually have shallow floor toms (such as 16x13).
- The deepest toms have **symmetrical** or **square sizes** (12x12), but these haven't been popular for quite a few years.
- Then there are drum kits designed for easy transportation, a tight sound, or both. They feature **very shallow** toms (such as 12x5).
- And there are also drums that have **no shells** at all, each drum consisting of nothing but a round frame, a tuning system and a head.

Toms come in a variety of depths: a 12x10 power tom and a 'standard size' 12x8

Floor toms

The most popular floor tom is the 16x16, followed by the 14x14, but some companies make 18" and 15" models as well. Floor toms usually have square sizes, though extra deep ones (15x17, 14x16) are also available, and most 18" floor toms are 16" deep. An 18x18 would hardly leave any room between the bottom head and the floor, thus preventing the sound from developing and making for a sluggish response.

Feet off the floor

In the late 1980s and early 1990s, many drummers, especially in fusion, replaced their floor toms with slightly shallower drums that were mounted on a stand. This increases the response as well as the available floor space. The 14x12 and 15x13 are the most popular sizes for these drums, which are usually referred to as *hanging* or *suspended floor toms*.

TOM HOLDERS

Most drummers mount their rack toms on the bass drum rather than using separate stands or a drum rack. Many of today's tom holders or *tom mounts* incorporate some kind of *isolated mounting system* which prevents the hardware from absorbing most of the sound of the drums.

Tubes and rods

A lot of entry-level kits come with tom holders modelled on a very basic yet effective Pearl design, which basically consists of two sets of two tubes, each with a tilter in the middle. Another basic design involves one centre post and two L-shaped rods for the toms. Most other holders are somewhere between these two systems.

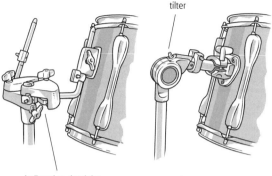

tilter

ball-and-socket joint

Two different tom holders

Toothless tilters

The tilters are most often *ratchet tilters* which use two sets of interlocking 'teeth', but *toothless tilters* offer finer and faster adjustment. *Ball-and-socket joints* are also fast and accurate, allowing omnidirectional adjustment using just one thumbscrew.

Which one?

Apart from the ease of adjustment, the actual differences between tom holders aren't that great and bad ones are hard to find. Tom holders nearly always come with small metal clamps that 'memorize' your settings, allowing you to set up fast, whilst also adding to their stability. Some names for these clamps, which are also used on hi-hat pedals and elsewhere, are *memory locks*, *key locks* and *stop locks*. Some tom holders have hexagonal arms, which help to stabilize the drums, whilst others allow you to mount a third holder next to the ones for the toms.

Lost vibrations

If the tom bracket is attached directly to the shell you may experience a loss of tone and sustain when you mount the drum on its holder. Try this test: tune a tom, play it and listen to its sound whilst holding it by the hoop. Then mount it on the tom holder and listen again. If you hear a difference the reason is that it's not only the heads that vibrate, but also the shells. And if the bracket is attached directly to the shell of the drum a lot of the vibrations will be absorbed by the mass of the metal bracket and the tom holder.

Isolated tom mounting
In the early 1980s drummer Gary Gauger introduced a solution to this problem. With his Resonance Isolation Mounting System (RIMS) the toms are mounted on rubber, hanging from their tension rods. The original tom bracket is attached to a side plate. Many companies have come up with their own solutions collectively known as isolated mounting systems, whilst others use copies of the original RIMS.

Tom mounted with RIMS

Floor toms
Though floor toms may also benefit from isolated mounting – some brands do offer special floor tom legs to allow greater resonance – the effect on rack toms is much larger.

LISTEN UP
Once you know what you're looking for, it's time to start listening to the drums. Here are some tips for testing and comparing.

The same heads
Whenever possible, compare drums with the same or similar heads. If you don't, you're comparing heads more

than drums, since the heads are the biggest factor in determining the sound. Also, make sure the drums have similar tunings. This involves more than tuning them to roughly the same pitch, as you'll find out in Chapter 9.

The best heads

If you want to hear the drums as they really sound it's best to use medium-clear heads on the toms and a medium-coated head on the snare drum, and both without any muffling. Muffling makes drums sound nice and fat, but also very much alike. Refer to Chapter 7 for more on head types.

The difference

In terms of sound, what does more money actually buy you? Generally, higher-priced kits offer what's often referred to as a richer sound, with lots of lows, mids and highs, all nicely balanced. Balance gives a drum its character, and also allows it to speak well – on a good kit you will hear each note on each drum, even during high-speed fills. And drums that speak well also project well. Their sound will cut through other sound, so you're less likely to need amplification when playing with a band.

Timbre

The mix of lows, mids and highs determines the instrument's timbre, or the 'colour' of its voice. Whether it sounds fat, dark, bright, transparent, solid, sweet, subdued or harsh, this is the timbre – and this is where it really comes down to taste. There's no such thing as a typical rock drum, a typical jazz drum or a typical studio drum: what makes a 'typical' fusion kit or a 'typical' heavy metal kit are the sizes, heads and tuning of the drums, not the drums themselves.

Sustain, attack and response

When testing drums, play them as loudly and as softly as you intend to do after purchasing. Listen to the balance between the attack (the initial sound of the stick hitting the head) and the tone (that which follows). Also, listen to how the drums respond. If·you do quiet gigs your drums should be able to sound at their fullest even when played softly.

Tuning

Tune the drums the way you plan to play them. If you've got a sensitive ear you can also compare tuning ranges. How high and low will the drums go before losing their tone? You may find that expensive drums are harder to tune than budget instruments – it takes more time and experience to balance out the wider sound range of high-end drums.

Many factors

A drum's sound is determined by everything attached to it and by every aspect of its production. The number of plies, the shell thickness, the bearing edge, the type of wood, the finish, the hoops, the heads, the lugs... the list goes on. So, in the end, despite all the technical specifications, the most important thing is simply how a kit sounds and feels as a whole.

Too long

After testing drums for fifteen minutes or so, you'll probably find it hard to hear all the subtle differences between one kit and another. If so, take a break or come back the next day – you'll most likely be in a much better state of mind to make a sensible judgement. Also, avoid trying to compare too many instruments at once. Instead, select two or three snare drums, for example, and play each in turn; then swap the one you like least for another, and so on.

SECONDHAND

Pretty much everything that has been said above also goes for secondhand drums and drum kits. However, there are a few things to pay particular attention to when testing used instruments.

- Check that everything's **complete and in working order**. Are all the hoops, lugs and tension rods present? A used bass drum may have lost its front head and everything else that's supposed to come with it.
- Check if the drums **tune properly and easily**. If not, check the heads, and that the shells and hoops are perfectly round and level.
- The condition of the **finish** often indicates how carefully the kit has been treated. Check wooden hoops, especially,

and see whether the snare drum has scratched the lacquer off the left rack tom.

- Drum kits can live to a **ripe old age**. Twenty or thirty years is no problem provided they have been looked after. Expanding used kits with matching drums may be a problem, however, especially in the lower price ranges.

- Older used kits sometimes come with **single-headed toms**, also known as *concert toms*. These usually have a short and not very resonant sound.

- European drums from the 1960s or earlier may have **metric sizes**. Replacement drum heads can be made to order, but they're expensive.

- The lug nuts of older kits may be kept in place by **springs**, rather than by nylon inserts (see page 34). These springs tend to vibrate along with each beat unless they have been muffled with small pieces of foam plastic. Alternatively, every spring may be encased in a piece of plastic tubing.

- Remember that the **brand name on the heads** says nothing about the brand of the drums.

An old-fashioned lug with a spring

6. HARDWARE

The key requirements for stands, pedals and all other hardware items are pretty basic: they should be stable, sturdy, easily adjustable and noiseless. But there's a lot more than that to know about the subject. Read on...

If a drum kit comes with hardware, check out all the separate items. Some cheaper kits come with nice stands but have awkward pedals, for instance. Others offer less quantity (the stands are not as heavy) but more quality (everything works better and pedals move faster). It's important that your hardware should be sturdy, but if you're not a very heavy hitter you probably don't need really heavy, bulky stands.

Hardware sets

If hardware is not included, most brands offer two or three hardware sets from which you can choose. You're always free to go for a different brand, of course, but using accessories and instruments from one brand may only improve the looks of your kit as everything is likely to have the same styling. Tom holders usually come with the drums, so they're covered in Chapter 5.

BASS DRUM PEDALS

The snare drum is your most personal drum, the ride cymbal is your most personal cymbal and the bass drum pedal is your most personal piece of hardware. Good midrange pedals that will take you through any gig are available for around £50–125, but you can spend much more.

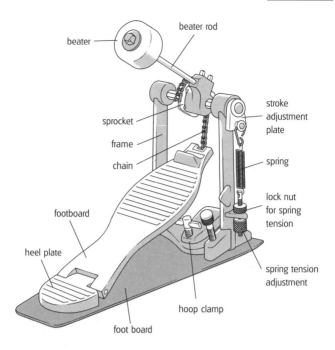

beater rod

beater

stroke
adjustment
plate

sprocket

frame

chain

spring

lock nut
for spring
tension

footboard

heel plate

spring tension
adjustment

hoop clamp

foot board

A bass drum pedal

Spring tension

Every bass drum pedal comes with an adjustable spring. The higher you set the tension, the harder you'll have to work to depress the pedal and the quicker the beater will come back. Usually, drummers with a heavy foot technique use a heavier spring tension, whilst players with a lighter technique set their pedals with a lower tension. As always, though, there are numerous exceptions to this rule. Some pedals offer some type of locking adjustment screw that secures your tension setting.

Chain or strap

Pedals come in two basic versions: they're either *chain-driven* or *strap-driven*, referring to the connector that runs from the footboard to the sprocket. The two types feel different, and not just because of the chain or strap, but because the entire assembly is usually different. On most chain-driven pedals the chain runs over a round sprocket with the main axle passing through the sprocket's centre. This makes for a very even feel, or *action*.

Eccentric sprocket

Strap-driven pedals, on the other hand, often have what's known as an *eccentric cam*, which means the footboard travels a little further and the action is lighter. There are also chain-driven pedals with eccentric sprockets, as shown below, which generally provide an action somewhere between the two standard types.

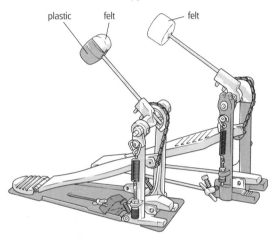

plastic   felt   felt

A bass drum pedal with a regular chain drive system (left) and one with an eccentric sprocket. Also note the different beaters.

Adjustable action

Some pedals feature an adjustable action, which is different from an adjustable spring tension. Adjusting the action changes the distance your footboard has to travel, and this influences not only the feel of the pedal, but the resulting sound as well. Also, you can alter the action without changing the way that the beater comes back to you.

Worth the money?

If you're shopping for a pedal, try experimenting with the settings of one with an adjustable action. This will help you find out whether you prefer a heavier or a lighter action – and once you decide what you like, you may realize you don't need a pedal with an adjustable action at all.

More than one

Some drummers use different pedals for different styles of music. For example, a player may choose a pedal with a light action when playing *heel up* (pressing the pedal down somewhere in the middle of the footboard) and another, with a heavier action, when playing *heel down* (with the entire foot on the footboard using all the leverage the pedal provides).

Chains and teeth

Chain-driven pedals used nearly always to be fitted with a metal sprocket wheel, but these have gradually been replaced by less noisy, felt-lined wheels, which come either with or without a couple of 'guiding' teeth. If there are any teeth on a pedal, check that the chain matches them properly. A double chain adds stability to a pedal and its action, but as chains are unlikely to break, life expectancy isn't necessarily increased by making them twice as heavy.

Stability

The more stable a pedal is, the more efficiently your energy will be translated into sound. A *base plate* (also known as *pedal plate* or *stabilizer plate*) will help improve stability, and also reduce unwanted noise. However, pedals with base plates take up more room in transportation, and they're a bit harder to attach to the bass drum if the thumbscrew is

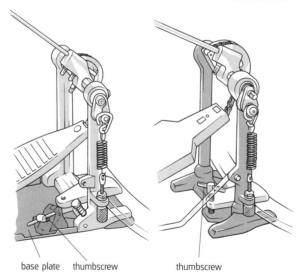

base plate   thumbscrew   thumbscrew

A pedal with a base plate and a thumbscrew mounted to the side of the footboard (left) and one without a base plate with a thumbscrew under the footboard (right)

situated under the footboard. Thankfully, thumbscrews are increasingly placed on the side of the pedal.

Beater and footboard angle

The greater the angle of the beater, the longer the stroke it can make, and therefore the louder you can play. Many pedals offer three or four beater angle positions corresponding to the number of holes in the *stroke adjustment plate*, or *spring swivel*. If there's a slot instead of a couple of holes you can make finer adjustments. When changing this setting, the footboard angle often changes too – increase the stroke and the footboard will rise up, which may not be what you want. Unfortunately, there are only a few pedals on which both angles can be set independently.

The beater

The beater influences the sound of a bass drum significantly and also affects the feel of the pedal. The harder the beater, the clearer or brighter the attack will be and the more need there is for a protective pad on the bass drum head. Beaters come in felt, plastic and wood – some even have interchangeable surfaces – and felt beaters, the most popular choice, are available in various different hardnesses. Cheaper models are usually on the soft side, producing a mushier sound with less attack, and they generally wear down faster. Beaters also differ in weight, which has a considerable effect on the feel of the pedal. If you want to play with a heavier beater than the one you own, special weights are available, which can be attached to the beater rod so as to speed up the action.

Bearings

A good pedal only moves when – and where – it's supposed to. If there's any unwanted play or give in the moving parts of a pedal, things can be more difficult to control, and your movement won't be passed on as efficiently to the drum head. More importantly, any type of play will only get worse. Various production techniques, such as the use of bearings in the heel joint, help to prevent play from developing.

Smooth

The action of a bass drum pedal should be smooth and

noiseless. To test a pedal for this, put it on a table or counter and move the footboard up and down with your hand. This way you'll hear any unwanted noise. Also, you'll feel even the slightest irregularities in the action.

Spurs, spikes or Velcro
To keep them from moving forwards, pedals usually have either retractable *spurs* or *spikes*. Other models have a coarse type of Velcro (known as 'industrial Velcro') or rubber underneath the base plate.

Double pedals
So-called double bass drum pedals allow you to use both feet to play the bass drum. If you plan to purchase one, always feel for play in and around the shaft that connects the two pedals. Hold the cam or the sprocket of the secondary pedal, and try to move the secondary beater. If there's any play, again, it's bound to get worse. Unfortunately, very few pedals come with ball bearings in the U-joints of the shaft, although these do prevent play in the long run.

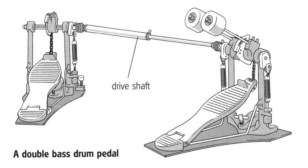

drive shaft

A double bass drum pedal

HI-HAT PEDALS
You can judge a hi-hat pedal in much the same way as you would judge a bass drum pedal. However, the number of adjustments is much smaller.

Spring tension
Some budget hi-hat pedals come with non-adjustable springs. If the spring tension is too light for the cymbals you're using the action will be slow. If it's too heavy you'll

have to work too hard. So you're usually better off getting an adjustable one; they start at around £50.

The tilter

When closing your hi-hat cymbals you may hear a sound something like 'zomp', rather than 'chick'. Usually this is the result of *air-lock*, the air between the two cymbals acting as a restrictive cushion. To prevent this, the bottom cymbal can be usually be tilted, most commonly by adjusting a screw that angles a metal washer under the bottom cymbal. There are also special hi-hat cymbals that have been designed to prevent air-lock; see Chapter 8 for more.

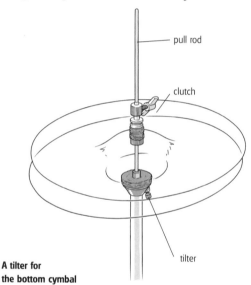

pull rod

clutch

tilter

**A tilter for
the bottom cymbal**

Clutches

The top cymbal is attached to the *pull rod* by a *clutch*. Even a very basic clutch will do in most cases. Some clutches are more expensive because of their looks; others feature a special type of bolt giving them an extra grip on the pull rod, or a system preventing the nuts (and eventually the top cymbal) from coming loose.

Drop-lock clutches

A variation on the regular design is the *drop-lock clutch*, which features a special release mechanism. When you hit a catch, the top cymbal is released and drops onto the bottom cymbal. This allows you to continue playing the hi-hat with your sticks whilst using your hi-hat foot for something else, such as the remote pedal of a double bass drum pedal. When you next press down the hi-hat pedal the drop-lock clutch picks up and 'locks' the top cymbal again. This is very useful for some styles, though when you let the top cymbal drop your closed hi-hats may sound a bit 'loose', as the top cymbal is resting on the bottom one with only the force of its own weight, instead of being pressed down by your foot.

Felts

The harder the felts that hold the cymbals, the brighter the sound can be. Some clutches and bottom cymbal holders have rubber instead of felt rings – again, the harder the material and the smaller the contact area, the brighter the resulting sound.

Swivel feet and two-legged hi-hats

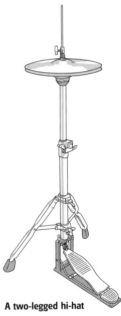

A *swivel foot* allows you to swivel the legs around the base of the hi-hat stand, providing additional flexibility in set-ups with double bass drum pedals. As an alternative, there are hi-hat stands with just two legs, a base plate taking the place of the third. On some of these pedals, the base plate and footboard can be folded up for transportation. If not, they take up a lot of space.

A two-legged hi-hat

Remote pedals and X-hats

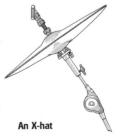

If you want an extra pair of hi-hats you have two options. One is a *remote hi-hat pedal* operated by means of a long cable. With one of these you can position the cymbals pretty much anywhere you like, and the additional pedal is operated with the same foot as the regular hi-hat pedal (see page 121).

An X-hat

Solution number two is an *X-hat*, or *closed hat*; these come without a pedal and simply clamp the two cymbals together. A built-in spring allows you to create both tight and loose hi-hat sounds.

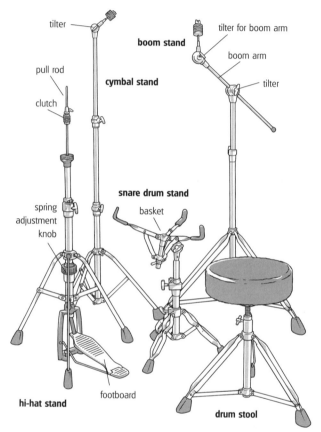

tilter

boom stand

tilter for boom arm

boom arm

pull rod

cymbal stand

tilter

clutch

snare drum stand

spring adjustment knob

basket

footboard

hi-hat stand

drum stool

STANDS

Even the most basic stands usually do what they're supposed to, but there are still some issues to think about. For example, most stands have double-braced legs, and unless you're a heavy hitter you may consider whether you really want to carry that extra weight around each time you move your kit.

Speed of set-up

When checking out a stand, make sure it's quick and easy to extend and retract the tubes, and fold the legs in and out.

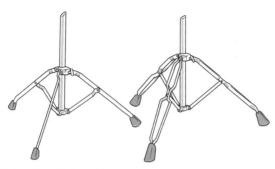

Single and double braced legs

Some stands have extremely 'fast' thumbscrews to speed-up the process of setting up and taking down – with these, one turn is often enough to secure each clamp.

Toothless tilters

Toothless tilters on cymbal stands, as with tom holders, offer infinite adjustment and are faster to work with than the traditional ratchet tilters, which have two sets of inter-locking teeth (the finer the teeth, of course, the finer the adjustment). Ball-and-socket joints, as found on some snare stands, can be adjusted in any direction.

Wing nuts

If the stem of the cymbal tilter has an unthreaded top (known as a *pilot*), this will help to prevent the wing nut from falling off when you're tightening or loosening it. Alternatives to the traditional wing nut range from sleeve/nut combinations to clamps and so-called *T-tops*, all of which save you set-up time and prevent you from tightening down cymbals too much (see also pages 96–97).

Some alternatives to the traditional wing nut

Boom stands

Some boom stands come with counterweights. Usually, you can do without this extra mass, but if you're in doubt, consider a stand with a detachable counterweight. There are also convertible boom stands: if you don't need the boom arm, you can make it retract into the upper tube.

Snare drum stands

The snare drum should be secured between the rubber grips of the basket, but tightening the basket too much may stifle the sound of the drum. Most snare drum stands hold 13" drums as easily as 14" ones, and some even take a 15" as easily as a 12". It's worth considering the maximum and minimum height settings of a snare stand, especially if it might be used for very deep or very shallow snare drums.

Two parts

Some cheaper cymbal stands consist of two parts, rather than three. These have one drawback: the parts need to be longer, so they may not fit in a hardware case or bag. Other than that, they're fine.

RACKS, CLAMPS AND STOOLS

Drum racks help you to set up every item of your kit (including microphones) in exactly the same position every time. And they can make setting up a lot faster too.

Set-up with drum rack

They also transform the look of your kit, from a forest of stands to three or four sturdy legs. The bigger your kit, the more useful a drum rack will be – for standard five-piece set-ups, and for drummers who like to vary their set-up, traditional stands often make more sense.

Multi-clamps

Multi-clamps or *adapters* allow you to attach drums, cymbals, cowbells and other equipment to a drum rack or a cymbal stand. They vary from very basic affairs to clamps with multiple angling possibilities – those with hinge joints are the easiest to work with. Some clamps can hold only thicker tubes, whilst others also hold thinner rods, as used for some toms.

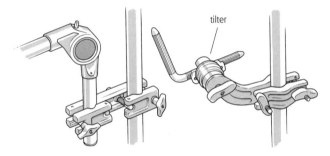

Multi-clamps

Stools

A decent stool, or *throne*, will cost you somewhere between £30 and £140. On the most basic models, the height is set by inserting a bolt into one of a series of holes in the upright tube. If this doesn't allow for the exact height you want, consider simply drilling an extra hole in the tube, though be very careful when doing so as the drill bit may slip off the metal causing risk of injury. Other stools have threaded rods, which allow for exact height adjustment. With one of these, ideally, turning the seat should not alter its height.

Mind your back

If you can't set your stool to the exact height you need, or if it wobbles, your back will probably tell you something's wrong after a few hours of playing. However, do be careful, as sometimes people ignore minor discomfort only to find out in a few months that they've permanently damaged their backs. A back support (preferably an adjustable one) may be a good idea, especially if you play long gigs.

The seat

Traditionally, drum stools have rather small, round seats. Saddle-shaped seats may offer more comfort as well as assisting blood circulation in the upper legs. And fabric-covered seats, instead of the usual vinyl, help prevent a sweaty feeling. Picking the right seat hardness is largely a matter of taste.

7. HEADS AND STICKS

Drum heads are the most important factor in determining the sound of your kit, so it's worth knowing about the various types available. There are plenty of options when it comes to sticks, too, though often the best sticks are simply those you don't notice using.

If you compare a drum kit to a hi-fi, the heads correspond to the speakers. They are the element that sets the air in motion and actually creates the sound.

Different heads

With a hi-fi it's much easier to hear the difference between two sets of speakers than between two amplifiers. Likewise, it's a lot easier to hear the difference between two identical drums with different heads and tunings, than two different drums with the same heads and tunings.

Budget heads?

Many budget kits come with budget heads that dent easily, are hard to tune and don't sound very good. Replacing them with professional heads will noticeably improve the sound of a kit. The most audible improvement usually comes from changing the batter heads of the toms; expect to pay around £30–50 for three of them. If you've got the cash, replace the snare drum batter as well, followed by the bass drum batter – it all helps. And for total perfection replace the resonant heads too.

Medium

The most basic drum head has a clear, single ply of medium-heavy polyester film. Such heads, which are popular on toms, both on top and bottom, produce an open, regular and true sound with lots of sustain. Some examples are Remo Ambassador, Evans G1 and Aquarian Classic Clear. Basically, medium drum heads all have the same thickness, often indicated as 1000 gauge or 1 mil., equalling 0.01" or 0.25mm.

Medium coated

The most popular snare drum batter head is a medium head with a white coating. This coating muffles the head slightly, whilst also helping to produce a bright, crisp attack. It also roughens the surface of the head, which is necessary for playing with *brushes* (see page 69). Coated heads are sometimes also used on toms and bass drums.

Two-ply

Heavier players often use two-ply heads, especially on their toms and bass drums. These heads sound fatter, warmer and shorter than one-ply heads and they also last longer. Some examples are the Remo Pinstripe, the Evans G2, Aquarian's Performance II and the Attack Thin-Skin-2. Don't use these heads as bottom heads because this will kill the drum's projection. A popular combination for toms is two-ply heads on top and thin heads on the bottom. Two-ply heads are usually made up of two 700-gauge plies, which amount to a thickness of 0.36mm.

Dots

If two-ply heads sound too muffled, you might consider *dotted heads*, single heads with an extra piece of drum head material in the middle. These pieces, or dots, affect the sound, making it slightly deeper and more focused, and they also strengthen the head at the main point of impact. Dotted heads are mostly used as tom batter heads. Because drum heads with regular dots are difficult to play with brushes you can also get batter snare drum heads that have a dot on the reverse side.

Thin

Thin single-ply heads (700 gauge or 0.18mm) are used primarily as resonant heads for toms. When combined with two-ply batter heads they project better, with increased brightness. The basic polyester material is the same as used for other types of head – it's often referred to as Mylar, though this is actually a trade name of the Dupont manufacturer.

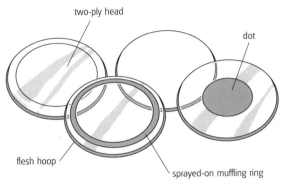

Different types of heads

Snare-side head

Snare drums need special *snare-side heads*. These heads are extremely thin to allow the snares to bounce off them and create that unique snare sound. Most medium snare-side heads are 300-gauge. If you only play very quiet gigs you could try a 200-gauge model (only 0.05mm), and if you're a heavy drummer try a 500-gauge.

drums	toms batter	toms resonant	snare batter	snare resonant	bass batter	bass front
head types						
transparent medium	●	●			●	●
coated medium	●	●	●		●	●
two-ply / dotted	●				●	●
thin		●				
built-in muffling ring			●		●	●
snare-side head				●		

Different heads and the types of drums with which they can be used

Muffling rings

There are various ways to add muffling to drum heads. In the late 1990s the built-in muffling ring became increasingly popular on snare drum (batter) and bass drum heads. These very thin rings are held by their edges against the inside of the head and don't alter the attack sound because they bounce off the head when you strike it. The muffling effect comes after the attack, slightly drying out and shortening the sound. Some bass drum heads come with two rings, one of which is removable. There are also sprayed-on muffling rings, though these have only a very slight effect on the sound.

Other types

There are many other types of heads as well as those described above. The Evans Hydraulic, for example, includes a touch of muffling oil between its two plies. (Other two-ply heads may look as though they contain oil, but actually the 'oily' colours you see are made by the refraction of light, not by oil.) There are also drum heads that, for muffling purposes, have a ridge or a series of tiny holes around their circumference. Then there are heads made to re-create the softer feel and complex sound of calf skin heads, and extra-strong drum heads made of Kevlar fibres, as used in bullet-proof vests. And these are just a few examples.

Two heads, one drum

Finding the right heads is a matter of experimentation, time and patience. A good technique for comparing tom heads is to put one type of head on one side of a tom and another on the other side, and tune them to the same note. The result will be different from playing with a proper resonant head, but nevertheless you will be able to note the characteristic differences between the two heads.

Another brand

If you change your drum kit you may want to consider changing your heads too, as different heads sound better than others on different kits. And don't limit yourself to one brand and type – your toms may sound best with Brand A, and your bass drum with Brand B. The ideal combination for your snare may be C on top and D below. Similar types of head from different brands will behave differently: a two-ply head from one brand, for example, might sound different or dent more easily than a similar head from another.

Three more brands

As well as the brands of drum head mentioned above, some drum companies have their own professional drum heads, such as Ludwig, Premier and Sonor.

STICKS

Drumsticks come in hundreds of different sizes and types. Within all these variations there are four basic types that every brand supplies: the light and slim 7A, the versatile 5A and 5B, and the hefty 2B. Their details are shown in the chart on the next page.

Some basics

Whether you're likely to prefer heavier or lighter sticks depends on a number of things. Generally speaking, heavier drummers use heavier sticks for a heavier sound. Heavier cymbals require heavier sticks to get the metal to move, and deeper drums require heavier sticks for pretty much the same reason. However, heavy sticks are not good for thin cymbals because they're more likely to crack them.

Exceptions

There are, however, many exceptions to these rules. Whilst playing softly is more difficult with heavier sticks, some drummers do so anyway, because they prefer the sound or feel of a heavier stick. And there are drummers who manage to sound surprisingly heavy with surprisingly light sticks. Also, whilst most drummers play everything with one type of stick, others use different types for different groups, gigs or songs.

Beginners

If you've only just started playing, you will probably find it hard to appreciate the minute differences between the many types of sticks available. It may be good to start with one of the standard types – a 5A or a 5B if you like things a little on the heavy side or a 7A if you have smaller hands. A 2B is generally considered to be a bit too heavy for beginners. Once you know which one of the four main types suits you best you can 'fine-tune' your selection by going through the many variations on offer. Some guidelines for choosing sticks are provided in the following paragraphs.

The differences

The best sticks are the ones that make you feel, play and sound the way you like to – they're the sticks you don't even notice using. Sticks basically differ in thickness, length, weight and balance. A thicker stick will feel 'meatier' in your hand and produce a meatier sound. The longer a stick is, the easier it descends (good for playing loud), but the slower it ascends (bad for playing fast). Also, a longer stick provides you with more reach. Obviously, both length and thickness also influence a stick's weight.

Balance

Balance has to do with weight distribution. A short taper and a thick neck move the weight forwards making the stick feel and sound heavier than it is. Whether a stick has the 'right' balance largely depends on where you hold it and how you play.

tip neck   taper   shoulder   shaft   butt

Not the same

Every stick maker has its own idea of what the 'standard' 5A, 5B, 7A and 2B sticks should be, but generally these standard types are pretty similar. The following chart shows their average dimensions.

type	weight	length	diameter	neck
7A	45 grams	15.75"/40cm	0.530"/13.5mm	0.235"/6mm
5A	50 grams	16"/40.5cm	0.570"/14.5mm	0.255"/6.5mm
5B	55 grams	16"/40.5cm	0.610"/15.5mm	0.275"/7mm
2B	65 grams	16.25"/41cm	0.640"/16.5mm	0.295"/7.5mm

Average dimensions of 'standard' stick models (rounded off)

Feels like more

As you can see, everything increases just a little at a time, yet a 2B feels completely different from a 7A. This also explains the astounding number of models available.

'Rock' and 'Jazz' are sometimes regarded as standard models too, but such models vary more from one brand to the next than the four standard types described above. The Rock type sold by one brand may be as much as 50 percent heavier than that of the next brand.

Hickory, maple, oak

The weight, feel and sound of a stick are also influenced by the type of wood used. Most sticks are made of hickory, a flexible yet strong wood, but other woods such as maple are also common. Maple sticks weigh less and have a lighter sound than hickory, so if you like the feel, but not the weight, of a thick stick try a similar model in maple. Similarly, if you like the weight of a stick but it's too thin, a similar model in maple may be perfect. If you're a heavy player, you could try oak – it's heavy, dense and strong, and makes for a bright sound.

The tip

The material and shape of the *bead* or *tip* of a stick also affects the sound. Most sticks come with wooden tips, though many have nylon tips, which last much longer and sound brighter. Most stick manufacturers offer distinctive shapes for nylon and wood tips on their otherwise identical models.

Tip shape and size

Bigger tips make for a bigger sound by generating more highs and lows. Small tips yield a very controlled sound, but they also cause dents in the drum heads more easily. Oval tips offer the largest range of sound variations on your ride cymbal, letting you alter the tone considerably just by changing the angle at which you play.

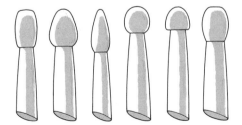

Every tip gives a different sound

Feels different
Most sticks have a lacquer or wax finish. Which you prefer is very personal and depends largely on your particular type of skin and sweat – a stick that's perfect for one player may quickly become unusably slippery in the hands of another. There are also differences between various types of lacquer, of course.

Get a grip
If you have suffered from slippery sticks, try sticks with a different coating, or get yourself some drummers' gloves. Alternatively, wrap some tape around your sticks – special stick tape is available. Some other options are unfinished sticks, sticks with knurled grips, sticks with built-in rubber grips, and sticks with thicker grip areas.

Equal weight, equal sound
Most drummers look for a pair of sticks that are equal in weight and sound, which usually means trying them out one by one. Some brands offer computer-selected pairs that are matched extremely well. Even then, however, you may want to select a few pairs that all have similar weights and sounds.

Weight differences
Not many drum shops have a postal scale, though such a device speeds up the process of selecting a large number of sticks of similar weights. Generally, if you can't feel the weight difference in the shop, you probably won't feel it when you play, but 'identical' sticks, whether prepacked or not, often vary 10% or more in weight – and that you can feel.

Checks
When checking for straightness, roll the sticks over a tabletop or counter. When checking for sound play them one by one on a similar surface, or use one stick to play the other. Some drummers even play their head to check that the sticks produce the same pitch.

Non-wood
Besides wood, there are loads of sticks available in other materials such as carbon fibre. Some say that they last

longer and are more consistently made than wooden sticks, whilst sounding as good and feeling roughly the same. Certainly some come very close. Carbon-fibre sticks retail for around £25 a pair.

Wire brushes

Drummers don't always play with sticks – there are various alternatives that offer a very different sound and feel. The most common are *wire brushes*, or just *brushes*, which are mainly used by jazz drummers. A standard brush consists of a rubber handle with many thin steel wires sticking out of it. Usually there's also a thicker piece of wire with a loop at the end protruding from the back of the handle, which allows you to choose how far out you want the wires to be, letting you create a range of different sounds, especially on cymbals. Wire brushes differ in the exact gauge of wire they use – a heavier gauge produces a heavier, broader and coarser sound – and there are also brushes with different materials, such as nylon, instead of wire. Another thing that varies is the material of the handle, which may be rubber, wood or plastic. Rubber is by far the most common, even though in most cases it becomes pretty sticky after a while. Naturally, there are also variations between brushes in terms of balance, weight and overall length.

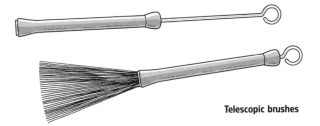

Telescopic brushes

Multi-rods

Another alternative to sticks are tightly bundled wooden or plastic dowels – commonly known as *multi-rods* – which produce a sound somewhere between sticks and brushes. Multi-rods come in many varieties, with more or fewer dowels, heavier or lighter dowels, and so on. On some types the sound can be influenced by moving a plastic collar up or down the dowels. A tip: most types will sound good if you don't play too softly.

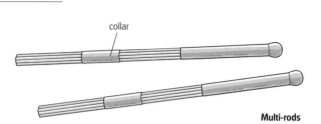

collar

Multi-rods

Mallets

Just like sticks, *mallets* come in lots of different styles, many of which are designed for specific percussion instruments, such as timpani or xylophone. Timpani mallets have big, soft heads and work really well for long rolls on cymbals, as well as for creating special effects on toms.

Brands

Some of the established stick, brush and beater manufacturers are Agner, Premier, Pro-Mark, Johnny Rabb, Regal Tip, Rimshot, Shawstix, Vater, Vic Firth and Zildjian. Each of them produces dozens of different models and, in some cases, different brands as well. This explains why you may come across two identical sticks with different brand names.

8. CYMBALS

Cymbals look very simple, but they're not. A good cymbal is in fact very hard to make, which explains why decent models can cost a lot of money. This chapter takes a look at the various sorts, and provides tips on choosing and combining cymbals.

Finding the best cymbals is a bit easier if you know a little about why these bits of metal sound the way they do. The following section deals with this; if you'd rather choose cymbals using your ears only, skip to the tips on page 73.

Series

Most manufacturers make cymbals in various different price ranges. They also make series of cymbals arranged by sound characteristics, or series that are aimed at certain styles of music. Cymbal catalogues can be useful for information on what to expect from a certain series.

Sounding names

Many cymbals have names that may help you in making a first selection. Names like Power, Full, Dark and Fast speak for themselves, more or less. But weight indications, such as Medium, aren't as informative as they sound: if you were to compare ten 16" medium crash cymbals from various brands and series, you'd hear ten quite different sounds.

Heavier, larger, higher

Many elements influence the sound of a cymbal. Four of them are easy to discern: weight, diameter, cup size and profile.

- If you had two similar cymbals, one slightly **heavier** than the other, the heavier one would sound both higher and longer. It would also have a slower response – so a heavy crash, for example, needs a heavy blow to really crash.
- A **larger** cymbal has a lower pitch and a longer sustain than a similar but smaller cymbal. The larger cymbal also requires more power to respond.
- **Cup size** influences volume, response and the amount of *overtones*, or *harmonics*, in the sound. Overtones make a cymbal sound richer. A larger cup makes a cymbal respond faster and produce a louder, more full-bodied sound.
- A cymbal with a **higher bow** will have a higher pitch and a slower response than the same cymbal with a flatter profile.

Interrelated

All these parameters are interrelated. For instance, a heavier cymbal may sound lower than a lighter one of the same size because it has a lower profile.

Hammer marks

The way a cymbal has been worked also has an effect on the sound. In terms of the hammering, the more regular the pattern of hammer marks (the dents on the surface of the cymbal), the more 'regular' and clean the sound will be. An irregular pattern, such as created when hammering a cymbal by hand, helps produce a darker and more complex, 'irregular' sound.

Grooves

The circular grooves found on most cymbals enhance the spread of the sound. Cymbals that have no grooves (*unlathed cymbals*; see Chapter 13) have a tighter, drier, more compact and more metallic sound. Regular grooves help produce a clean, even or regular sound, whilst uneven grooves enhance the complex character of many hand-made cymbals.

Alloys

As a cymbal consists of one part only, the material it's made of plays a major role in determining the sound. Five basic alloys are used in cymbal production:

- Budget cymbals are often made of **brass** or **nickel-silver**, the first producing a warmer sound than the second.
- The oldest cymbal alloy is a bronze containing 20% tin and 80% copper. This metal, known as **B20**, is used for the professional series of Zildjian, Sabian, UFIP and Turkish Cymbals.
- The lower tin content of **B8** gives this bronze alloy a slightly reddish tint. Its somewhat tighter sound can be heard in cymbals such as the classic Paiste 2002s, in most professional Meinl cymbals, and in many lower and mid-range series of other brands.
- Paiste's own **Sound Alloy** is closer to B20 than to B8.

'Identical' cymbals

Two cymbals of the same series, type and size may sound a lot more different than they look. The variations between 'identical' cymbals are generally bigger where B20 is used, and more specifically in cymbals that feature an irregular hammering pattern. For this reason, even if you're sold on one particular type of cymbal, listen to and compare several examples of that cymbal before deciding which one to buy.

Budget cymbals

Cymbals often come in prepacked sets, especially but not exclusively in the lower price ranges. If you want to be sure that you'll enjoy your purchase for a long time, unpack the set and test each cymbal. There are major sound differences between low-budget series – you may well like the ride cymbal from one brand or series and the crash from another. However, buying separate cymbals is more expensive, even within the same series.

RIDE CYMBALS

The attack sound (the *ping*) of a ride may vary from a very penetrating, clean sound to something rather dark, thick and dry. Generally speaking, louder music demands a ping with more definition, which you'll get best from a heavier cymbal. A good test is to crash the cymbal and then play a ride beat at the volume at which you intend to use the cymbal – if you hear the individual beats from the very start, you're on the right track. Listen to the sound of the ping: it may sound high or low, dry or wet, thick or thin, solid or delicate.

The cup

The cup has a very tight, pronounced sound. Nevertheless, it shouldn't sound like a different instrument when compared to the sound from the rest of the cymbal. Play the cup and listen to what the rest of the cymbal does. Does it sound when the cup is played or is it only the cup that you hear no matter how hard you play it?

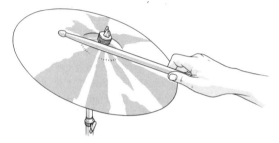

Playing the cup

Crash-rides

Many 18" and bigger cymbals can be used for riding and crashing. Dedicated *crash-ride cymbals* are available, and can be a solution if you can afford only one cymbal, but professional crash-ride cymbals are rare. Many jazz and fusion drummers use their cymbals for riding as well as for crashing. Typically, they choose relatively thin cymbals with irregular hammering – these produce a wide array of overtones whilst having sufficient definition to be used for ride patterns. These cymbals are usually not marketed as crash-rides, however.

Ride sizes

Most drummers use 20" or 22" ride cymbals, but you can get them in 18", 19" and 21" as well. Smaller and bigger rides are rare.

HI-HAT CYMBALS

When checking out hi-hat cymbals play them in lots of different ways. Depressing the pedal should produce a good, definite *chick* sound – if it's followed by a sweeping tone don't buy the cymbals. Playing them in their closed position should produce a nice, tight sound; if they sound 'hollow' don't consider them. Also, open the hi-hats and play them with sticks to see how fast they respond.

Clutches and stands
Testing and comparing hi-hat cymbals is easiest if you have a few clutches to hand, allowing you to switch sets of cymbals quickly. Better still, use a couple of hi-hat stands, one for each pair of cymbals you're comparing.

Bottom and top
If you need your hi-hats to produce a very definite 'chick' sound, go for a pair that has a considerably heavier bottom cymbal. And if you're a very loud player, consider using both heavy top and bottom cymbals. Don't hesitate to mix tops and bottoms from various pairs of hi-hats if the shop owner allows you to do so – some cymbal fanatics even mix cymbals from different types, series or brands.

Air-lock
To prevent air-lock (see page 54), some brands make bottom cymbals with corrugated edges or extra holes.

Hi-hat sizes
Most drummers use 14" hi-hats, but 13" are also pretty common. Smaller sets, typically 10" and 12", are mainly used as additional hi-hats on an X-hat (see page 56) or a remote hi-hat (see pages 55 and 126). Larger hi-hats are rare.

CRASH CYMBALS
The most important thing when shopping for crash cymbals is to pick those that produce most of their highs and lows immediately when struck, when played both lightly and heavily. Apart from this, it's mainly down to personal choice: you may like a crash that cuts through everything and sustains for a long time or prefer something more subtle which disappears right after the initial attack.

Shop versus stage
In a shop, crashes always seem to sound longer than they will on stage. The louder the music you play, the larger this

difference will be – some cymbals seem to ring forever when struck hard in a shop.

Too thin

Drummers with a heavy attack sometimes buy crashes that are too thin for the music they play. This is because in the shop thinner crashes sound more pleasant than the power crashes they actually need.

Different

At a distance, and when used in a band, crashes tend to sound much more alike than they do in a shop. So although you need to choose cymbals that form a good set, it's generally worth going for more extreme contrasts between your crashes than you may think is suitable when in the shop.

Crash sizes

Apart from 16" and 18" crashes – the most popular choices for any style – there are crashes in even and uneven sizes from 12" up to 22".

EFFECT CYMBALS

As well as the standard ride and crash cymbals, there's a wide range of so-called *effect cymbals* available, which can be used for creating all sorts of different sounds.

Splashes

Splashes are small, fast crashes, which produce a 'splashy' sound with quite a lot of attack but hardly any sustain. They come in sizes between 6" and 12", and in a wide range of weights. Heavier splashes won't 'splash' unless they're hit extremely hard; really thin ones respond incredibly fast, but break quite easily if played with real force.

Chinas and China types

Chinese cymbals were originally made to scare the enemy, and they have an upturned edge that helps produce an aggressive, rough and exotic sound. The Western variations on this theme, with a regular 'Turkish' cup, offer a sound that is mellower and less 'dirty' than the very affordable but also more fragile Chinese design.

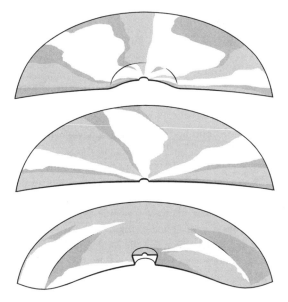

The profiles of a regular cymbal, a flat ride and an original Chinese cymbal

And more...

Flat rides, which have no cup at all, produce a delicate, very controlled ride sound. *Sizzle cymbals*, as their name suggests, make a sizzling sound. They have two or more loose rivets strung through them, usually near the edge, which vibrate when the cymbal is struck. Then there are special cymbals for orchestral percussionists, cymbals that are no more than a big cup, China splashes, cymbals with holes, cymbals with square cups, cymbals with jingles and many more variations.

BUYING TIPS

If you're a first-time buyer, start by picking your ride or hi-hats, depending upon what you use most for timekeeping. Crashes, splashes and effect cymbals can come later. Whatever cymbals you're buying, here are a few useful tips:

- **Take any cymbals you already use with you.** This way you can hear whether the new ones 'fit in'. Don't be scared to freely mix brands and series.
- When testing cymbals, use **your own sticks** or a similar pair.

- When checking out a selection of cymbals, only **compare two or three at once**. Discard the one you like least each time and replace it with another. Replace the one you like least. And so on.
- If possible, listen to your final selection **as part of a drum kit**. And try and use them the way you do when you play for real.
- Bring along **another drummer** and have them play the cymbals as well. You'll get a second opinion and you'll also be able to hear the cymbals from a distance.
- If there are no other drummers around close the **one ear** that's in the general direction of the cymbals, and then play them. This will give you a closer idea of what they'll sound like live, in a band setting.
- And the ultimate test? Use the cymbal **with your band**. Most shopkeepers won't let you, though, for obvious reasons.

Secondhand cymbals

There are plenty of used ride and hi-hat cymbals for sale. After all, they hardly ever break, they're quite expensive and many drummers go for a change or upgrade from time to time. Here are some tips for secondhand cymbal shopping:

- **Cracked cymbals** will invariably crack further. Never buy them.
- Check secondhand cymbals for **invisible cracks**. Play the edge of the cymbal with your finger. Hold the cymbal close to your ear and listen for the slightest buzzing or rattling.
- Avoid cymbals with a **worn-out hole** (known as a key hole). They have probably been played without a cymbal sleeve (see pages 96–97).
- Cymbals that **shine very brightly** around the hole have probably been mounted too tight, which increases their risk of cracking.

A cymbal with a worn-out key hole

Old-style cymbals

As long as you follow the above points, you should be able to enjoy your used cymbals as much as if you'd bought them new – they can last for decades. Some drummers even prefer old cymbals (especially the famous and rare old Ks from the formerly Turkish Zildjian factory). They're so popular, in fact, that most brands offer special series to re-create the cymbal sounds of the 1950s and 1960s, with names like Traditional, Original, Classic or Nostalgia.

9. TUNING AND MUFFLING

Drums can't sound out of tune in the same way as most instruments, yet tuning is essential in making a drum sound as good as possible. It only takes seconds to make a great drum sound like a box, but it takes longer to tune it to its best. The basics are set out in this chapter, which also includes tips on muffling.

It's up to you how you want to tune your drums. You may want them high and tight, low and fat, or anywhere in between. Yet every drum has a certain tuning range – tuning above it will make the drum choke and tuning below it will kill its tone. Every drum can also be tuned to a point, somewhere in between these extremes, at which each element of the instrument seems to come together. When you reach it you'll hear the longest, fullest, biggest and most musical tone that drum is capable of producing. A quick guide to tuning is provided in this chapter, but learning to tune effectively and quickly takes time, so be patient.

One per string

Tuning many instruments is quite straightforward. A guitar, for example, has one tuning mechanism per string, and each string can be tuned either too low (*flat*), too high (*sharp*), or just right.

Five or more per head

Tuning drums is a bit more complex, as there are five to ten tension rods for each head, and you have to create an even tension at each rod. What makes things really difficult is that adjusting one rod also influences the tension at the other rods.

Drums and kits

Tuning a whole kit not only requires each head to have an even tension, making it in tune with itself, but also that there's a balance between the top and bottom heads of each drum. Finally, you also have to tune the drums relative to each other, so creating the intervals (tonal distances from drum to drum) that you like.

12", 13", 16"

The sizes of the drums dictate these intervals to some extent. So if you have a kit with 12", 13" and 16" toms there will be a large interval between the 13" and the 16". Trying to make it smaller by tuning the 13" quite low and the 16" quite high will result in two drums that do not sound as though they're parts of the same instrument: the smaller drum will have a fat sound, while the bigger one will sound thin.

Drum keys

Pretty much every brand has its own model of *drum key*, but every key fits every drum. Drum keys are usually provided with a small hole so you can attach them to a key ring. Apart from regular keys there are various types that help you tune or remove heads faster, such as *speed keys* and *ratchet keys*.

A regular drum key, a speed key and a ratchet key

BASIC TUNING

To get most from this section take a 12" or a 13" tom (these are easier to handle than floor toms, and easier to tune than most 10" toms) and remove the heads. Put the drum on a folded towel or a piece of foam plastic so you won't damage the bearing edge.

Worn-out heads

Drum heads should be replaced when they become dented or worn out. You can tell a worn-out head because it will no longer look level when viewed from the side – as shown in the illustration below. Such heads have lost most of their elasticity and therefore most of their sound, too. While the heads are off, you may also want to clean the hoops, the inside of the drum, the lugs and the rods.

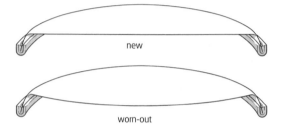

new

worn-out

A new and a worn-out drum head

Basic tension

Put the batter head on the drum. To create a basic even tension all around the head, use your fingers to tighten all the tension rods as much as you can. This may be difficult, though, especially if your drums have very short tension rods, in which case use a drum key to turn each rod so far that the underside of its square head just touches the hoop. Whether you're doing it by hand or using a key, it helps if you deal with the rods two-by-two, tightening opposite rods simultaneously. The diagrams on the following page suggest tuning orders – on a drum with six tension rods per head, for example, start with lugs 1 and 2, then do 3 and 4, and finally 5 and 6.

Higher and higher

Now slowly increase the tension, tightening the rods half a turn at a time in the order shown on the diagrams overleaf (or one of the many variations). When the head starts to produce an agreeable tone you're nearly there.

The pitch

Continue tightening the rods, perhaps in quarter turns now. Meanwhile, lightly tap the head at each rod, about an inch from the edge using your drum key, a fingertip or a stick. As soon as you start hearing the pitch you're looking for, it's time for the hard part: fine-tuning. This is all about making sure the head produces the same pitch across its surface at every tension rod.

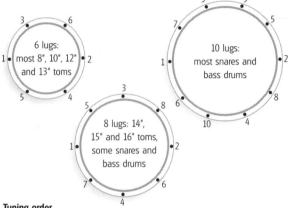

6 lugs:
most 8", 10", 12" and 13" toms

10 lugs:
most snares and bass drums

8 lugs: 14",
15" and 16" toms,
some snares and
bass drums

Tuning order

FINE-TUNING

No matter how precisely you've tuned the head so far, you'll find that it produces a slightly different pitch at each rod. To even this out, and to create a uniform pitch and tension, takes time. Here are a few tips:

- Hearing the head's pitch is easier if you **place a finger in its exact centre**. Just touch it, don't push. This way, tapping at the lugs will produce a clearer tone.
- Take as your starting point the one rod at which **you best like the pitch**. This is now lug number 1. The pitch will probably be the same at the opposing lug, which becomes lug number 2.
- **Compare this pitch** to what you hear at lugs 3 and 4. If they sound too low (flat), tighten them a little. Note that the pitch at 1 and 2 goes up when doing this, so loosen them up a tiny bit. Drum tuning is about creating a balance: give a little here, take a little there...
- Don't worry too much if you're having trouble getting 3 and 4 to sound the same pitch as 1 and 2. The pitch at opposing lugs often sounds identical, but that **doesn't**

mean the tension is the same at those lugs. Try tightening 2 and lowering the tension at 1, or the other way around. If that doesn't work try the same with 3 and 4.

- When comparing two pairs of rods, also **listen to the pitch at the other rods** from time to time. If the tension at 5 is much too low on an eight-lug drum, you'll never get 1 and 3 to sound the same.

- If you want to lower the pitch at a certain lug don't just unscrew it. Instead, **always tune up**: first, loosen the tension rod until the pitch is clearly too low, then go up from there.

- **If you can't get the drum properly tuned**, don't panic. Take the heads off and start all over again. Before doing so, take a break, or consider asking an experienced drummer to help you.

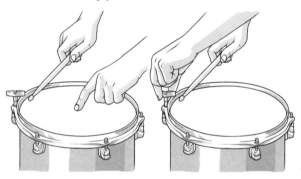

Placing a finger in the middle of the head, tapping and adjusting the relevant tension rods

Bottom heads

Once the batter head has the pitch you want, you're ready to mount the bottom head. Basically, you have three tuning options: tuning it to the same pitch as the batter head, to a higher pitch or a lower pitch.

- Tuning the heads to the same pitch creates a long, clear, clean and even tone.

- A higher-sounding bottom head will make for a tone that's brighter and livelier, with increased cut and projection.

- Tuning your bottom head lower will result in a deeper sound – more of a thud – with reduced sustain. But the tighter top head helps the stick rebound and accentuates the attack.

Which?
The only way to find out what you (or your drums) like best is to try each option. When experimenting, don't overdo the pitch difference, as the drums won't sound very good that way. Also, a bigger difference increases the possibility that you'll get pitch bend, meaning the pitch of the drum will change after the attack.

Muffle the other head
When fine-tuning a head, always muffle the other one – put the drum on your drum stool or on a folded towel, for example. Also, when comparing the pitches of the batter and bottom head, always muffle one whilst hitting the other. Otherwise, both heads will sound similar, even when they're not tuned the same, as their pitches will tend to blend and sound like one.

Mounting the drum
If your drum kit doesn't include an isolated mounting system (see page 44), mounting a well-tuned tom on its holder may drastically reduce its sustain, resonance and tone. There are two solutions. One is to fine-tune the drum when mounted (in which case be sure to mount the second rack tom, too, as they're bound to influence each other). The problem with this is that the tom holder now dictates the tuning of the drum, which isn't really what you want. The other option is to provide your toms with an isolated mounting system, which shouldn't cost you too much these days.

Detuning
Drums detune because heads stretch quite a bit – especially when they're new – and because the tension rods become loosened, though some drums come with a system designed to prevent this (see page 34). Using softer, non-metal washers under the tension rods may help and will also make tuning easier. Lug-locks are among the various products available to help prevent de-tuning by 'locking' the tension rods.

Press down
Depressing a new, mounted head with your hands will help to take some of the initial stretch out of it. If you do this,

you'll notice the pitch drop considerably. Some drummers even stand on their bass drum heads for this purpose. It can be done – but be careful.

Actual notes

Some drummers tune their drums to actual notes, such as the 10" to a G, the 12" to an E and so on. If you want to try this out use a piano or other keyboard instrument as a point of reference. Electronic tuners tend to get confused when confronted with the many frequencies that drums produce – for drummers the ear is a more reliable tool.

The drum's pitch

Another point of reference for finding the right pitch for a drum is the shell itself. Take off the heads, put your arm inside the shell and balance it on one finger. Then tap it lightly, determine its pitch (you may want to use a piano for reference), replace the heads and tune them to the pitch you found. This often gets you pretty close to the point at which the drum sounds its best. Some players remove all the lugs and mounts before checking the pitch of the shell.

Tuning devices

There are special devices available that help you to tune by measuring the resistance of the rods or, more effectively, the tension of the heads. The latter are not cheap, usually costing £60–80, and fine-tuning is still up to you. However, they can make basic tuning a lot quicker. They can also help you to establish at which rod the tension is higher or lower, even when the pitch sounds the same. The Tama Tension Watch was the first device of this kind.

Adjusting

Try installing new heads with the logo in a particular position, perhaps between the same two lugs as the drum's badge. This way, if you take the heads off you'll always put them back in the same position, which can make tuning easier if the hoop or the head isn't perfectly round or level.

SNARE DRUMS

Fine-tuning a snare drum is a very similar process to tuning a tom. The major difference is that the heads will be a lot tighter. They have to be, otherwise the sound will be more of a 'boosh' and less of a 'crack'.

Ten lugs

Most snares have ten lugs, making it hard to keep track of the tuning order. A tip: write the numbers of the rods on the drum head, or on a ring cut from an old head.

Snare-side head

The snare-side head is pretty tight as well. However, because it is so thin, it's sometimes hard to determine its pitch. A starting point in finding the right tension is to put the tip of your left little finger against the top of your left thumb. Feel how tight the fleshy part below your thumb is, and tune the snare-side head so that it feels about the same. A very loose snare-side head will produce a loose, broad or thick type of sound, whilst tightening it will increase clarity and projection. Beyond a certain point, however, the head becomes too tight for the snares to respond well.

Stick in a stick

If the snares interfere with your snare-side tuning, temporarily separate them from the head. Very, very gently insert a stick under the released snares, moving it left and right, and rest its ends on the counter hoop.

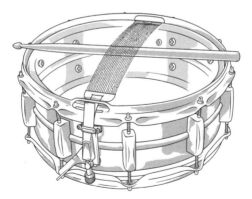

Make a 'bridge' for your snares

The snares

Adjusting snare tension is best done in the 'on' position. If you need the drum to sound good at all volumes, lightly tap the batter head whilst increasing the tension on the snares. As soon as they stop responding, and the sound becomes slightly hollow, loosen them a little. If you like to play really loud, though, you may want to tighten the snares up a bit more.

Detuning the snare-side head

The snares are supposed to 'snap' when you strike the drum, and then be quiet immediately. If they don't, one solution is to deliberately de-tune the snare-side head. To do this, loosen the four tension rods at either end of the snares and tighten the others to compensate. Now play the drum again, and it should sound as though you have tightened the snares, allowing you to loosen the snares a bit. When fine-tuning the snare-side head the tension should now be highest at 1 and 2, a bit lower at 5–8 and 6–7, and lowest at the other four rods.

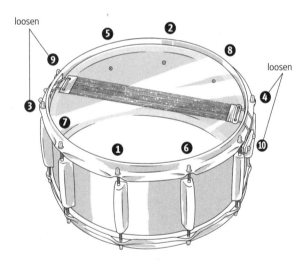

Loosen these four tension rods a little and tighten up the rest to compensate

The other way around

On some snare drums this trick only works if you do it the other way around: tighten the rods at either end of the snares and loosen the others. How much you'll have to change the tension depends on pretty much all the factors mentioned so far, so experiment.

Snare buzz

Snares are not supposed to respond when you play a tom or your bass drum, or when the rest of the band starts up – yet they do. Don't worry too much as the resulting snare buzz is heard mainly by you, the drummer. However, if it gets too loud or distracting there are a few things you can try.

- If your snares resonate when you play one of your toms, try **adapting the tuning of that tom**. You can change its pitch or keep the pitch the same by loosening the bottom and tightening the top head a little – or the other way around. If you still have no luck you may have to change the tuning on your snare drum, or do both.
- **Check the snares**. They're supposed to touch the snare-side head over their entire length. If you doubt their condition, take them off, and see whether they rest flat on a table top. And if they don't, replace them.
- The **distance between the snares and the drum's hoop** should be equal on both sides, and the strings or straps should pull evenly, both right and left. Contrary to what you might expect, this is not the case on many new snare drums.
- The snare strings **shouldn't be too thick**. Shoelaces, for example, are. Your local drum supplier should stock special snare strings.
- Finally, remember the most simple and obvious solution. If you're not using your snare drum – during a quiet intro to a song, for example – you can always kill the buzz by temporarily **releasing the snares**.

Different snares

To a certain extent, your snare drum sound is also influenced by the exact type of snares that are fitted. Indeed, snare sets vary considerably – there are sets with heavier and lighter strands, with strands made of harder or softer material, with less or more windings per inch, and with less or more strands. Heavier strands, more strands and more windings all make for a 'thicker' sound, whilst strands of a harder metal make the sound a little brighter. Bear in mind that not every set of snares will work with every drum. An extra-wide set, for example, with thirty or more strands, makes no sense on a drum with a relatively narrow snare bed.

BASS DRUMS

Most drummers tune their bass drums really low, often to a point where the heads only just lose their wrinkles. If you increase the tension you'll get more tone and less attack, until the drum starts to choke again. Really high tunings are mainly used by jazz drummers on small 18" bass drums.

Interval

As for the interval between the two heads (and other tuning principles), bass drums generally behave like toms. That said, one difference is that most bass drums are muffled and many have cut-out front heads. A tip: the less muffling you use, the more important it is to apply even tension to both heads.

MUFFLING

For bass drums tuning and muffling often go hand in hand. Many drummers also muffle their snare drums, and though toms are generally left to sound wide open, they too are sometimes muffled.

Muffling the bass drum

There are many ways to reduce a bass drum's tone and ring. Here are some examples.

- For light muffling, check out bass drum heads with **built-in muffling rings** (see pages 63–64).
- A much cheaper alternative is using a **felt strip** about one third of the way along the head(s). These strips bounce from the head at the moment of attack, just like a muffling ring. Felt strips can also be used on the front head only, combined with heavier muffling of the batter head.
- You can buy special **bass drum pillows** that bounce from the head with impact. These allow a full-sized attack sound but muffle what comes later.
- A **rolled-up towel**, taped in the angle where head(s) and shell meet, is a lot cheaper. It also sounds different as it always stays in contact with the head.
- The Remo Muff'l is a **polystyrene ring** held against the circumference of the head in a plastic U-shaped 'tray'. This tray also covers the precious bearing edges of the drum. It's very effective, especially on batter heads, when

combined with a resonant head that's only slightly muffled.

- Another old-fashioned yet effective and inexpensive muffling method is to partially fill the drum with **shredded newspaper or small pieces of polystyrene**.
- For a really short sound try putting a strip of **1" or 2" thick polystyrene** around the inside of the shell, just touching the head(s). Or simply put a pillow or blanket inside the drum.
- If band members complain that your bass drum resonates too much just **detune one or both heads**. It's fast, effective and doesn't cost anything, and it's also great if you need a tighter sound for just one or two songs.

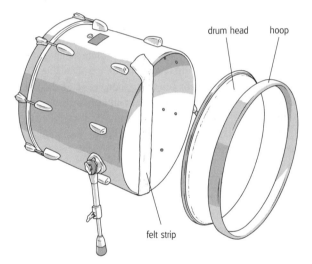

A bass drum with felt strip

The front head

For a long time, bass drums were played without the reso-nant front head. This effectively reduces resonance as well as sustain. A less drastic solution is to cut a hole in the front head, or buy a pre-cut (*ported*) front head. If the hole is in the middle of the head, opposite the beater, the effect will be similar to having no head at all. Even if it's just a small hole, the sound will fly straight out.

Smaller hole

By contrast, a small (4–6") hole near the edge hardly

affects the sound at all. Holes like this are often made so that a microphone can be put inside the drum. They also give access to the inside of the instrument so that, for instance, you can adjust the muffling. As a general rule, the larger the hole, the more attack and the less tone and resonance the sound will have. A hole also reduces the rebound of the batter head – the larger the hole, the less rebound.

Removing the entire head
Removing the entire head may result in rattling lug nuts, a deformed bass drum shell and damaged bearing edges. It's better to cut out most of the head and leave just two or three inches around the perimeter.

The template and the edge
Many drummers use a cymbal as a template when cutting a hole, though there are special templates available. You can also get products to cover the sharp edge of the hole; a do-it-yourself alternative is to cut a piece of thin rubber tubing open lengthways and mount it over the edge. Cutting drum heads requires a sharp knife – be careful not to damage your drums or yourself.

Attack
You can also increase the attack of a bass drum's sound by using a hard (wood or plastic) beater or by sticking a special self-adhesive pad on the point of attack. These pads are produced by various drum head manufacturers and other companies. As hard beaters are more likely to dent the bass drum head they are often used in combination with bass drum pads, which increase their attack even further.

MUFFLING SNARES AND TOMS
There are various ways to muffle snare drums and toms. Some work for both, others for snare drums only. Here's a look at the various options.

O-rings
An O-ring is a ring of drum head material that muffles the circumference of a drum, where most overtones, both

desirable and undesirable, are produced. O-rings are very effective on snare drums, and most snare drums come with one, though you can also either buy them separately or make your own (see below). They're rarely used on toms, however, as they muffle the sound too much and they may start buzzing because the heads move such a long way. An O-ring on top of the head creates a less open sound than a head with a built-in O-ring or muffling ring (see pages 62–63). As you'd expect, the wider an O-ring is, the more marked its effect will be.

Making your own
You can make something similar to an O-ring for your snare drum out of an old drum head. Use an old 14" head for a 14" drum: cut the middle 12–13" out and cut the flesh hoop off it. Take the batter head off the drum you want to muffle, place the ring you've cut over the bearing edge, put the batter head back on again, and tune the drum.

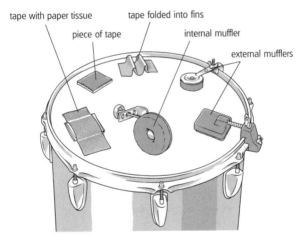

tape with paper tissue   tape folded into fins

piece of tape   internal muffler

external mufflers

Different mufflers

Tape
Duct tape (also known as *stage tape*, *gaffer tape* or *cloth tape*) works well on snare drums and toms. It's inexpensive, easy to apply and remove, and very versatile. First, locate the best point to apply the tape by gently running your finger across various places on the head's surface whilst playing. Then you have a few options. You can just stick a

piece of tape flat on the head, but folding it into fins increases the muffling, and it's even more effective when used to tape tissue paper to the head.

The outer edge

Unlike O-rings, tape and other small muffling devices don't muffle the entire outer edge of the drum where the high, crisp overtones come from. With these alternatives, rim shots and rim clicks will often sound better than had an O-ring been used.

Internal and external mufflers

Internal mufflers restrict the downward movement of the head. This is very noticeable and problematic on toms, which is why they're hardly used on them anymore. However, as these mufflers leave the head entirely open many brush players still like them on snare drums. *External mufflers* are flexible, fast and easy to work with. They're rare, however, one reason being that they don't move with a head as easily as tape does. They also take up part of the playing area and you usually have to remove them for transportation.

Tune, tune, tune

Snare drums and toms are often muffled to reduce the effect of clashing overtones produced by badly tuned heads. The better you tune a drum, the less you have to muffle it. More importantly, the more you muffle a drum, the less you'll be able to hear what you paid for.

Microphones

If your kit is about to be miked-up, spend extra time tuning it, as microphones are very good at picking up unwanted overtones. A properly tuned kit with an isolated mounting system for the toms is much less likely to get its heads covered in tape by a sound engineer.

Muffling and volume

The only way to muffle your drums so they won't be heard by your neighbours is to stuff them with polystyrene or cover them with rubber discs (see page 15). The types of muffling discussed in this chapter will barely reduce the overall volume of sound you produce.

10. SETTING UP AND MAINTENANCE

Drummers are among the few musicians who can set up their instruments to fit them perfectly. This chapter offers some basic tips on setting up, and also covers keeping everything in working order and taking your drums on the road.

If you want to save energy and gain speed and control in your playing, set up your drums so that at any time you are able to reach every piece of your instrument without really stretching your arms. The drums in the illustration on page 4 are set up this way.

The stool

As a starting point, adjust the height of your stool so that the tops of your thighs are parallel to the floor. If you're young – or small – this may prevent you from reaching your toms and cymbals. Buying a smaller kit (see page 12) is one option, but you could also try removing the second rack tom so you can lower your most important cymbal, the ride, to a playable height.

The pedals

Position the pedals so that your shins are angled slightly forwards. And set the length of the spurs on the bass drum so that the bottom of the front hoop is raised one or two inches from the floor.

The snare drum

Put the snare drum at such a height that the batter head is one or two inches higher than your thigh. If you use a *matched grip* (gripping both your sticks the same way) tilt the drum towards you slightly. Drummers who use a *traditional grip* often tilt it to the right, towards the floor tom.

The toms

Set the floor tom at the same height as the snare drum, and angled slightly towards it. The rack toms should be angled slightly towards you. If the angle is too steep, you'll end up with dented heads, because the larger the angle between stick and head, the more easily the head is dented. Position the toms so that the lower sides of the batter heads are roughly four to eight inches higher than your snare and floor tom heads. If set right, rack toms should not be so high that you need to raise your arms to play them, and not so low that you can't play rimshots on them.

The cymbals

Angle the cymbals towards you, as this makes them easier to play and harder to crack. Set your hi-hats about 4" higher then the snare drum, and position the stand so the cymbals slightly overhang the snare. The distance between the hi-hat cymbals determines how far your foot has to move up and down. Loud players often, but not always, have their hi-hats set higher and further apart.

Cymbal tips

If you're a heavy drummer and you use heavy sticks, you should probably use pretty heavy cymbals, as thinner cymbals are much more likely to break. Some heavy drummers do play pretty thin crashes without ever breaking them, but this requires a good playing technique. For one thing, such drummers don't avoid playing through their crashes (following *through* with the wrist or arm). Here are a few more tips:

• The stem of the cymbal tilter should always be covered with a nylon sleeve, or one of the many alternatives such as a piece of rubber tubing from a petrol line. Without such a tube, you'll create a keyhole in the cymbal and it may crack from the hole outwards. Also, the cymbal should always rest on a felt, leather or synthetic washer.

• Never tighten cymbals down. Crashes and splashes especially should be allowed a generous amount of give so they can go with the blow. Replacing the wing nuts with modern alternatives (see page 57) prevents over-tightening.

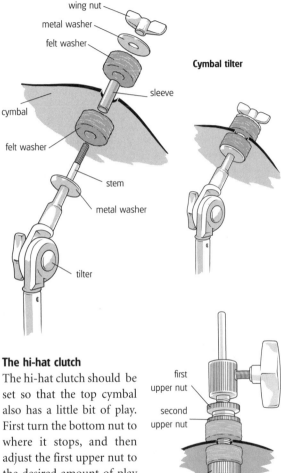

Cymbal tilter

wing nut
metal washer
felt washer
sleeve
cymbal
felt washer
stem
metal washer
tilter

The hi-hat clutch
The hi-hat clutch should be set so that the top cymbal also has a little bit of play. First turn the bottom nut to where it stops, and then adjust the first upper nut to the desired amount of play and secure it in place with the second upper nut.

first upper nut
second upper nut
bottom nut

A basic hi-hat clutch

Keeping things still
A piece of carpet is all you need to keep your bass drum and hi-hat from creeping away from you as you play. Use short-pile carpet – the softer the carpet is, the more it'll muffle your sound. The minimum size required is dictated by the area you need to accommodate your stool, bass drum, hi-hat and any extra pedals. If you arrive at a gig

and find you've left home without your carpet, one option is to use a piece of rope to tie your pedals to your stool.

Setting up fast

Using a piece of carpet can also save you time when setting up – simply mark the correct positions of stands, pedals and drums on it using tape (removable) or paint (unre-movable). Another tip for setting up fast is to use hose clamps on hardware items that don't have memory locks.

Left-handed players

Most kits are configured for right-handed drummers but if you happen to be left-handed, you have various options:

• You can **mirror the entire set-up** as shown below, but this is awkward if you share the kit with others. It can also make things less comfortable, as kits are usually configured for right-handed players.

A mirrored set-up

• As an alternative, **just move the ride cymbal** to the left side of the kit. Some right-handed drummers do this as well, having trained themselves to keep time with their (initially slower) left hand. This way, whilst keeping time on the hi-hat, they don't have to cross their arms anymore, as right-handed drummers have to in the standard set-up.

• Teach yourself to **play a regular 'right-handed' kit**, just as left-handed piano players and sax players (to name just two examples) play regular 'right-handed' instruments.

MAINTENANCE AND CLEANING

Keeping your drums in good working order is largely a matter of checking the nuts and bolts. When changing heads, check the bolts that keep the lugs in place. Loose-fitting parts may start buzzing and rattling, but never over-tighten them as that will restrict the vibrations of the shell. If you are about to be recorded, double-check your entire kit for any unwanted sounds, as microphones have a habit of finding sounds you've never noticed.

Oil

A few tiny drops of oil once in a while will keep your pedals moving smoothly. Stiff or jerky tension rods can also be cured this way unless you're dealing with jagged washers (which are often overlooked) or lug nuts.

More checks

Have a look at the snare strings (or straps) and replace them when they show signs of wearing out. The same goes for the sleeves on your cymbal stands. Also have a look at your pedals, checking that everything is as tight or as loose as it's supposed to be. Check, too, for play in parts that are not supposed to move and consult your dealer if you find any.

Cleaning

A soft cloth is all you need to keep your kit shiny, as long as you use it frequently. Glass cleaners work fine on covered drums and there are special cleaners for drums with lacquered, stained, waxed or oiled shells. Consult your dealer if you're in any doubt which one's right for your kit. Some players use regular furniture cleaners, though they can leave a greasy residue on the shells.

Cymbals

Use chrome polish for chrome-plated parts only and never for cymbals. If you want to be on the safe side, only use genuine cymbal cleaners, and follow the instructions closely as some of these cleaners are more abrasive than others. A few brands offer special cleaners for B20 or B8 bronze, the latter being less abrasive. Household detergents and water are also good for cleaning cymbals, but they don't make them shine. Always rinse and dry your cymbals thoroughly when you've finished cleaning them in this way.

ON THE ROAD

When you take your kit out of your home, it's important to keep it safe and to make sure that you have all the necessary spares with you. Here are a few tips.

- Treat your kit to a set of **cases** or **gig bags** (soft cases), preferably ones with some kind of shock-absorbing lining. Bags usually have shoulder straps and are easy to carry, but they're not always waterproof. Plastic cases usually are, but they're heavier and often cost more. Hard-shell flight cases offer ultimate protection, but they're usually heavy and expensive.

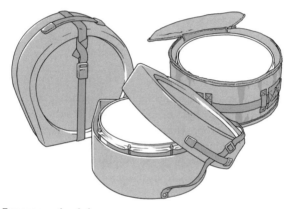

Two cases and a gig bag

- **Cymbals** also need to be protected – more than any other part of your kit in fact. Their edges in particular are very vulnerable. Some bags offer extra protection in this area, whilst cases usually have a centre bolt which keeps the cymbals in place, and hence protects their edges. Cymbal bags also usually come with separators, which keep your cymbals from scratching each other, and a shoulder strap.

- Consider insuring your equipment. Musical instruments generally fall under the **insurance** category 'valuables', meaning they won't automatically be covered by your home contents insurance. They may be covered in the home, but you'll almost certainly have to pay extra – often a great deal extra – if you want them to be covered when you take them out and about. There are special insurance policies available for musicians, though these won't necessarily be any cheaper.

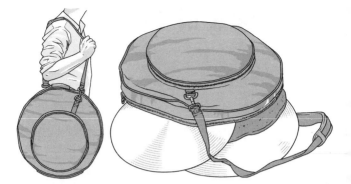

A cymbal bag with separators between the cymbals, handles and an adjustable shoulder strap

- In case your equipment ever gets stolen or lost, note down the **serial numbers** that you'll find on your drums (usually on the badges) and possibly also on your cymbals. This information is often requested by both police and insurance companies.
- Where possible, **avoid leaving your equipment unattended** – in cars or elsewhere.
- Whenever you're playing a gig – or even just practising – its worth having a few necessary **spares** with you. Firstly, always have some spare sticks, as they can break at any time. Brushes don't tend to break but they can shed their wires all of a sudden, so bring a spare set.
- Always have **spare heads** with you. Carry one, at least, for your snare (batter and snare-side head) and bass drum (batter). Keep them in the corresponding cases or bags, or in your car. Other items to bring are: snare strings or straps, a pair of pliers, a screwdriver, duct tape (for muffling, eliminating rattles and emergency repairs), cymbal sleeves, washers, tension rods, felt washers and a spare clutch (make sure it fits your pull rod, as they come in different sizes). If possible, also bring a spare bass drum pedal.
- If you play amplified most of the time you might consider buying **your own microphones.** There are special drummer's mikes available that attach to the hoops as well as systems for attaching mikes inside the shells.

11. BACK IN TIME

If the human voice is the oldest musical instrument around then drums must come a close second – they too have been around since prehistory. Even cymbals go back hundreds of years, though the drum kit is a relatively recent invention.

It probably wasn't long after humans discovered that hitting things sounds good that they realized hitting hollow things – such as hollow tree trunks – sounds even better. Presumably, the drum was born on the day that someone stretched an animal skin over the top of a hollow tree trunk and struck it. Since that day, hundreds of drums and percussion instruments have been invented.

Separate players
The very first jazz bands had two drummers. One played the snare drum, the second played the bass drum with one hand and the predecessor of the hi-hat with the other: the bottom cymbal, mounted on top of the drum, was played by hitting it with the top cymbal. This reflects the older tradition of classical orchestras, which have separate players for each percussion instrument and pairs of cymbals that are crashed together.

Pedals
Around 1909, William F. Ludwig came up with the first modern bass drum pedal. This allowed one drummer to play bass and snare drums simultaneously. A second beater rod hit a small cymbal mounted to the side of the pedal. This primitive device eventually made way for the

low-hat, or *Charleston pedal*, a lower version of today's hi-hat. It took another twenty-odd years for someone to lengthen the tube, raising the cymbals to a height where they could be played with sticks as well.

Toms

In the early days, drummers used so-called Chinese toms, which had tacked-on heads. Tunable toms were introduced some time in the mid-1930s, and drum kits haven't changed all that much since then.

temple blocks

A Carlton Ridgmount Console from 1935. Note the rack (on wheels), cowbells, temple blocks and the T-rods on the toms, with tacked on bottom heads. From the Collection of the Classic Drum Museum, England.

Heads

One of the few major changes in the history of the drum kit came in the late 1950s when plastic drum heads started to replace the traditional calf-skin heads. Calf skin sounds great but plastic heads are more consistent and reliable. Also, plastic is not sensitive to humidity; calf-skin heads, by contrast, need to be re-tuned every time the air gets a bit more or less damp.

Cymbals

The first cymbals were very thick and heavy, and were used in all kinds of rituals, processions and military music. The modern cymbal was born in Turkey in 1623, and is credited to one Avedis Zildjian I. Names like ride, crash and splash came much, much later. A 1948 catalogue, for instance, simply mentions twenty different sizes (from 7" to 26") in six different weights, from Paper Thin to Heavy.

12. THE PERCUSSION FAMILY

Drums and cymbals belong to a very large family of instruments, which includes every instrument that you strike to make the sound. It's called the percussion family, taking its name from the Latin word for striking, percussio. There are thousands of different percussion instruments around – this chapter introduces some of the most important and popular.

When non-classical musicians talk about percussionists they are usually referring to *Latin* percussionists, who play any combination of instruments such as congas, bongos, timbales, cowbells, shakers, rattles, scrapers – and more. The main drums, usually played with the hands instead of with sticks, are the tall congas and the much shallower,

timbales with cowbells

congas

higher-pitched bongos. Bongos are practically always played in pairs, whilst conga players – *Congueros* – use two, three or even more drums. Most congas and bongos still come with animal-skin heads, but plastic heads are used increasingly as time goes on. Timbales are typical Latin-American drums, which resemble metal snare drums with single plastic heads. They are played with sticks, nearly always in combination with one or more cowbells and usually a cymbal. Latin percussionists are found not only in groups that play Latin music, but also in those that play jazz, funk and other styles.

Classical percussion

Symphony orchestras have various percussion instruments, each of which is played separately. The most important elements are: snare drums, which are also referred to as *side drums*; a bass drum, which can be as big as 40" and is played with a beater not a pedal; a pair of cymbals, often called *clash cymbals*, which are crashed together; *timpani*, also called kettle drums and timps, which are huge, low-sounding copper-shelled drums with tunable single heads; and *mallet instruments* (see below). However, certain pieces also call for various other instruments, such as triangles, tubular bells, gongs, wood blocks, chimes and *suspended cymbals* (cymbals on stands). Classical percussionists are generally trained in all these instruments, though they often specialize in one or more.

Concert bands

Concert bands, or wind bands, have a similar percussion set-up to symphony orchestras, though they often also feature a drum kit – either instead of or as well as separate snare drum, bass drum and cymbals.

Marching bands

Marching bands have various percussion instruments adapted so that they can be carried by the person playing them. There are snare drums (often very deep models that are tuned extremely high), bass drums, mallet instruments and single-headed *timp-toms*, which take the place of the drummer's toms. All of these are fitted with straps, so they can be attached to the player. There are also usually pairs of cymbals, carried in the hands and crashed together.

Electronic drums

Electronic drums have more and more to offer each year, in terms of sound, playability and features. Most modern electronic drum pads have tunable heads that feel like real drums. What you play is picked up by built-in triggers that activate digitally recorded sounds, or *samples*. A sound module allows for many ways of editing these sounds to your liking. Though expensive, electronic drums are great for practising quietly, and they're also popular in studios.

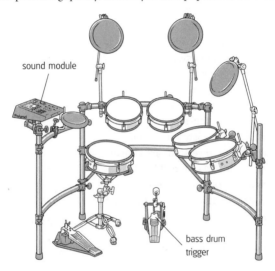

sound module

bass drum trigger

An electronic drum kit (Roland)

Acoustic, yet digital

Electronic samples can also be activated from a standard acoustic drum kit, by fitting it with microphones, special triggers or additional electronic pads. Some companies produce special small pads, specifically designed to be added to a regular drum kit.

Drum machines

Most drummers feel that drum machines are operated, rather than played. But they can be useful to practise with (they're more fun than a metronome) and in studio situations.

Mallet instruments

Melodic percussion instruments have metal or wooden

keys arranged like a piano keyboard. They are played with mallets – hence their other name of mallet instruments. If you play jazz, the mallet instrument you're most likely to come across is the vibraphone, which has metal keys and resonators with rotating metal discs that generate a vibrating sound. Marimbas and xylophones have wooden keys, and are mostly used in classical music, as is the bright-sounding metal-keyed glockenspiel. Marching musicians use lyras, which are like small glockenspiels.

Non-Western drums

Nearly every culture in the world has its own percussion instruments, and some of them have been adapted to the demands of Western percussionists. The *djembé*, for instance, is a popular rope-tensioned drum from Africa, with a distinctive hour-glass shape. Western versions are available with a tuning system like the one found on congas, a wood or fibre-glass shell and often a plastic head. Another African drum that has been adapted is the *talking drum*. This

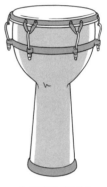

A modern djembé

drum is held under your upper arm as you play it, and by clenching your arm you tighten the ropes that connect the two heads, and hence change its pitch. Some other non-Western percussion instruments that have become popular in the West are Brazilian drums such as the low *surdo* and the high-pitched *repinique*, the Latin-American *cajon* (a wooden case that you both sit on and play) and many kinds of single-headed *frame drums*, which look like big tambourines without jingles.

Giant drums

Traditional Japanese drummers use sticks as thick as your wrist, and the biggest Japanese drum, the *odaiko*, is cut out of an enormous tree and weighs close to 500lb (over 200kg). The world's biggest bass drum was much lighter, but was truly huge: built in 1997 by the Dutch company Vancore, it featured 165" heads.

13. HOW THEY'RE MADE

There are many different ways to make drums, cymbals, heads and sticks: completely by hand, using computer-controlled machines or anything in-between. This chapter gives you a basic idea of the various manufacturing processes.

One of the main things you need in order to make a regular plywood drum is a mould, and a single mould costs as much as a decent car. Most drums are made up of wooden sheets that consist of three plies each, the grains running in alternating directions (*cross laminating*). These sheets are cut to very exact sizes, glued together, and then pressed around the inside of the mould. The drying process is usually speeded up using heat or microwave technology.

Pressing the wood around the inside of the mould

When the shell comes out, it is cut to length and the bearing edges are cut and sanded.

The finish

Lacquered drums have many coats, including stain, colour and one or more layers of clear, protective lacquer – and the shells are sanded or polished after every coat. The cover on covered drums is applied using glue or special double-sided adhesive tape. After the shell has been finished and drilled, the drum is ready to be assembled.

Readymade parts

Many drum manufacturers buy their shells readymade instead of producing them in-house. And most companies do not make their own lugs, hoops or other metal parts.

CYMBALS

Cymbals basically start out as flat, round discs. For their B20 cymbals (see page 73) most companies cast their own bronze. To do this they produce thick, round castings, one for each cymbal, and then roll them into flat discs in multiple steps. For most other cymbals the flat discs are made elsewhere. UFIP (see page 117) use moulds that already have the basic shape of a cymbal.

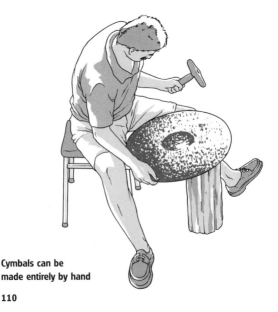

Cymbals can be made entirely by hand

The shape

Traditionally, cymbals are shaped using hammers, but only a few, mostly smaller, companies still do this entirely by hand. Most manufacturers use either mechanical hammers (rotating the cymbal under the hammer by hand), automatic hammers or computer-controlled hammers. The latter are even used for 'hand-hammered' cymbals in some cases. Sometimes, the cymbals are given an initial shape by pressing them before hammering, and the cup is nearly always made by a press.

Spinforming

Many less-expensive cymbals are *spinformed*: forced into shape against a rotating die. These cymbals are often recognizable by a wide, continuous, even groove on one side. In the late 1990s some companies also started using this technique on B20 cymbals.

Lathing

The fine grooves that you see on many cymbals are created on a lathe. The worker, or a machine, moves a hardened knife over the surface of the rotating cymbal. This process makes the cymbals shine and opens up the sound (in general, unlathed cymbals have a 'tighter' sound). A buffing process may be involved as a final step.

Finish

Most cymbals are finished with an ultra-thin coating, which makes them less susceptible to fingerprints and other stains. The coating is generally not thought to influence the sound, and it disappears over the years (sooner if you use a cymbal cleaner).

STICKS

Wooden sticks start out as timber that has been cured and cut down to square dowels about one inch across. A grindstone, or a knife with a blade the shape of a stick, removes exactly the right amount of wood along the length of the dowel whilst it's rotated on a machine. One way of finishing the sticks is to put hundreds of them in a big barrel and throw in some lacquer or wax. Spin the barrel for a while and the job's done.

HEADS

There are two basic ways of making heads. Remo, Evans and Aquarian use a kind of resin to 'glue' the heads inside the flesh hoop. Other companies fold the head around a square rod inside the flesh hoop before clamping it down. In all cases, the heads are cut out of large sheets of film, and the collar is formed using heat presses.

14. THE BRANDS

In this chapter you'll meet some of the main drum and cymbal brands, and a few smaller ones too. Some of the brands sell in all price ranges; others concentrate on either the budget or expensive ends of the market.

The drum market is dominated by nine major brands, which offer drum series in pretty much every price range.

 For many years Drum Workshop concentrated on high-end pedals and drums. With the introduction of the Pacific division in 2000, their products also became available in lower price ranges.

Ludwig goes back more than ninety years – it was this company that introduced the first modern bass drum pedal in 1909. The company's other legendary designs include the Supraphonic snare drum and the Speed King bass drum pedal.

MAPEX The Taiwanese brand Mapex arrived on the scene in the early 1990s, making it the youngest of the major brands. However, the company had been supplying both drums and parts to other brands for many years before introducing its own drums under the Mapex name.

 Pearl produced their first drums in Japan back in 1950 and have grown into a hugely successful company

since then. Perhaps their greatest single achievement is the Pearl Export, the world's best-selling drum kit – in 1995 the one millionth Export kit was produced. Various Pearl designs, such as their basic tom holder and bass drum spurs, have been widely copied by other companies.

PREMiER® The British company Premier has been around since 1922, and now has a huge product line including marching and classical percussion instruments as well as drum kits. Numerous Premier innovations, from double lugs to convertible boom stands, were introduced subsequently by other companies.

REMO® Drummer Remo Belli was one of the pioneers of the plastic drum head in 1957. The Remo company later introduced the wood-resin based Acousticon as the shell material for its own drums. Acousticon is also used for various other percussion instruments.

SONOR® The German Sonor company was founded in 1875. It is the oldest company in this list and has long been known for making pretty much every part of its kits itself. It is also known for its continued use of slotted tension rods, though these were discontinued on its low-budget, Asian-made kits in around 2000.

TAMA® The original name of this Japanese brand was Star, and this word still forms part of the names of all the company's series. Tama has always played a major role in hardware developments, such as the boom stand, the multi-clamp and the 'basket-less' Air Ride snare stand.

YAMAHA® Yamaha is one of the largest companies in the music industry. It produces a large number of other instruments besides drums (not to mention motor cycles, hi-fi systems, sailing boats and other products). Few modern kits have been on the market as long as their Recording Custom series, which was introduced in 1975.

American drum companies

Gretsch and **Slingerland** are two of the older American companies. Their first instruments date back to 1883 and 1921, respectively. Both companies offer mainly professional drums. **Rogers**, another brand with a long history, built its last US kits in 1983.

BUDGET PRICE RANGE

Many brands only or mainly offer drum kits in the budget and lower medium price ranges. Some of these brand names belong to Asian companies, others are owned by American companies that have their instruments made in Asian countries such as Taiwan and Korea. A few better-known examples are **CB Percussion**, **Cannon Percussion**, **Coda**, **Dixon**, **Peace**, **Rockwood**, **Sunlite** and **Taye**. Some of these companies offer a wider range of instruments and feature more original designs than others.

New brands

As with any other type of instrument, anyone can have their own custom brand of drums made. As long as the order is big enough, you can simply pick a shell design, select the lugs, hoops, holders, and spurs, have a logo and a badge designed and a new brand is born. Such brands sometimes represent good value for money, as little is spent on research and development, or on endorsements.

HIGH-END

If you want the best gear money can buy either look at the high-end series of the eight major brands listed above, or at the products of one the companies that concentrate on top-quality instruments only. Top-of-the-range drums don't come cheap, though: a single high-end bass drum can cost as much as three or four budget five-piece drum kits.

Shells and hardware

Hardly any of the high-end companies make their own shells, or their own hardware. Besides assembling and finishing the drums, their main activities are design, research and development. Usually, the shells will be supplied by either Keller or Jasper, two big US furniture companies who offer shells in pretty much every shape and size.

British drums

Britain doesn't have a huge number of drum manufacturers, but there are a few small British companies that produce high-end drums. Some examples are **Arbiter**, **Jalapeno**, **Noonan** and **Richmo**.

America

Many of the players in the high-end drum market are American. A complete list of these brands would include dozens of entries, but some of the most important examples are **GMS**, **Grover**, **Innovation Drum**, **Lang**, **Montineri**, **Noble & Cooley**, **Pork Pie Percussion** and **Spaun**.

Other countries

The number of high-end drum companies in other countries is considerably smaller, but there are quite a few around. One of the better-known examples is **Ayotte** from Canada, who make their own hardware and produce special tuning systems and Wood Hoop drums. Greece has **Gabriel**, France has **Capelle**, and Australia has **Brady** and **Sleishman**. In Italy, **Le Soprano** and **Tamburo** produce drums made with staves (strips of wood as used for congas).

Special drums

Some companies build drums that have some sort of speciality. For example, in 1997, the English company **Arbiter** introduced its Advanced Tuning System, which uses only one tuning bolt per head. This company also makes drums called Flats, with shells so shallow that they are pretty well flat. **Peavey**, well known for its amps and guitars, produces several series of drums with its patented Radial Bridge system. **Fibes** (Plexiglas), **Rocket** (carbon fibre), and **Impact** (fibreglass) are some of the companies that use alternative shell materials.

CYMBAL BRANDS

Though they look simple, cymbals are not at all easy to make – and that's just one of the reasons why the number of factories producing them is very small.

The city of Istanbul in Turkey is where the modern cymbal was invented nearly four centuries ago. The Istanbul company was founded in the early 1980s and by the turn of the new millennium six important cymbal brands were based in the city – Anatolian, Bosphorus, Grand Master, Istanbul Agop, Istanbul Mehmet and Turkish Cymbals. The cymbals manufactured by these brands are still made entirely by hand.

The German Meinl brand was founded in 1953 and for many years the company concentrated on the lower end of the market. In the late 1990s, Meinl's professional ranges expanded and the company also started producing an increasing number of other percussion instruments.

The Swiss cymbal makers Paiste made their name with the classic 2002 series, which is still around. In the late 1980s they introduced the Paiste Sound Alloy. This was a new alloy for professional cymbals. Paiste has always been widely represented across all price ranges.

Sabian (Canada) debuted with two series of professional cymbals in 1981. Since then they have gradually expanded their number of series, in all price ranges. Sabian is one of the few factories to make 'signature' cymbals, developed in co-operation with well-known drummers.

Having been an Italian brand from 1974 to 1986, Tosco started a second life in Canada in 1999 with a limited, single series of professional cymbals.

The merger of a number of small Italian cymbal makers led to the establishment of UFIP in 1931. There's still a lot of hand-work involved in their professional series, which were thoroughly revised in the 1990s.

The Zildjian company dates back to 1623 when Avedis Zildjian from Armenia discovered how to treat bronze in such a way as to make great cymbals out of it. Even after more than 375 years the current president is still a direct descendant of Avedis.

MORE CYMBALS

As with drums and other instruments there are more cymbal brands than there are manufacturers. **Camber** and **Headliner**, made by manufacturers mentioned above, are just two of the better-known examples. Low-budget Asian-made drum kits often come with Asian-made cymbals that either carry no name or the brand name of the drums. Specialist professional cymbal shops are very rare; one of them is **Spizz** (Italy), under whose name a series of low-budget cymbals is also produced.

British

The only British cymbals were made by Premier under the brand names **Zyn** and **Super Zyn** (standard and professional models respectively). Though they're no longer made, you may come across these cymbals when shopping secondhand.

Chinese cymbals

Most Chinese cymbals come from the province of **Wuhan**, where cymbals are still made the way they were decades ago.

15. SET-UPS

A drum kit can be as big or as small as you like – from a simple arrangement with bass drum, snare, hi-hat and a single cymbal to a huge set-up with three or more bass drums. The four kits in this chapter should give you some ideas, but they are just examples. After all, the definitive rock drum kit is just as imaginary as the definitive rock drummer.

STANDARD FIVE-PIECE KIT

Most drummers start on this basic, five-piece kit – and many stick to it. Combined with a similarly basic cymbal set-up, this arrangement will suffice for a wide variety of styles. A second crash cymbal, to the left of the ride, is often one of the first additions.

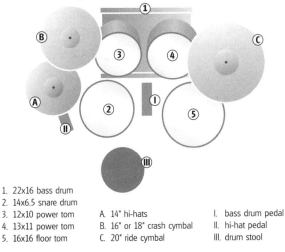

1. 22x16 bass drum
2. 14x6.5 snare drum
3. 12x10 power tom
4. 13x11 power tom
5. 16x16 floor tom

A. 14" hi-hats
B. 16" or 18" crash cymbal
C. 20" ride cymbal

I. bass drum pedal
II. hi-hat pedal
III. drum stool

NINE-PIECE ROCK SET-UP

The louder the music, the bigger the drums and the bigger and heavier the cymbals. Cymbals for hard-hitting drummers usually come with names like rock crashes, power rides and heavy hi-hats. And two-ply drum heads, which dent less easily than others, are a good idea. Tuning is generally on the low side.

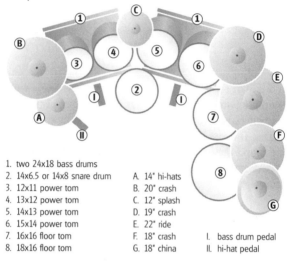

1. two 24x18 bass drums
2. 14x6.5 or 14x8 snare drum
3. 12x11 power tom
4. 13x12 power tom
5. 14x13 power tom
6. 15x14 power tom
7. 16x16 floor tom
8. 18x16 floor tom

A. 14" hi-hats
B. 20" crash
C. 12" splash
D. 19" crash
E. 22" ride
F. 18" crash
G. 18" china

I. bass drum pedal
II. hi-hat pedal

FOUR-PIECE JAZZ SET-UP

Many jazz drummers use four-piece kits in small sizes. These are often combined with two or three fairly thin, big, dark-sounding cymbals that are used both for crashing and timekeeping. One of these cymbals often has three or more rivets. The drums generally have coated, one-ply heads, often tuned to a high pitch.

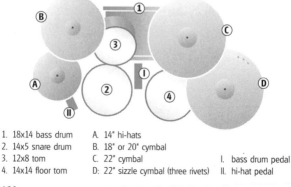

1. 18x14 bass drum
2. 14x5 snare drum
3. 12x8 tom
4. 14x14 floor tom

A. 14" hi-hats
B. 18" or 20" cymbal
C. 22" cymbal
D: 22" sizzle cymbal (three rivets)

I. bass drum pedal
II. hi-hat pedal

EIGHT-PIECE FUSION SET-UP

Fusion is a kind of cross between rock and jazz, and this is shown by the typical fusion set-up. The drums are smaller than those of the average rock kit, but there are more drums than most jazz drummers would use. Similar things can be said about the cymbals and the tuning, both of which are designed to supply a bit more power and definition than the average jazz kit. Heads can be either one-ply or two. Note the second snare, the mounted 'floor' toms, the cowbell and the double bass drum pedal. Also note the remote hi-hat pedal III, which is used to operate the hi-hat cymbals on the right (G).

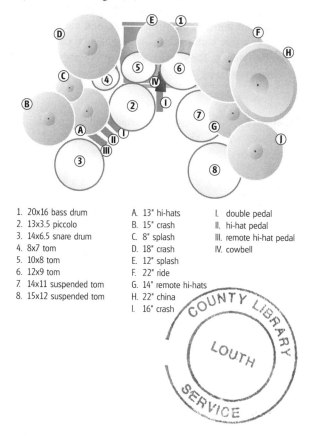

1. 20x16 bass drum
2. 13x3.5 piccolo
3. 14x6.5 snare drum
4. 8x7 tom
5. 10x8 tom
6. 12x9 tom
7. 14x11 suspended tom
8. 15x12 suspended tom

A. 13" hi-hats
B. 15" crash
C. 8" splash
D. 18" crash
E. 12" splash
F. 22" ride
G. 14" remote hi-hats
H. 22" china
I. 16" crash

I. double pedal
II. hi-hat pedal
III. remote hi-hat pedal
IV. cowbell

GLOSSARY AND INDEX

This glossary contains short definitions of all the drum and cymbal terms used in this book, and some others that you might come across in magazines, catalogues and other books. The numbers refer to the pages where the terms are used.

Acousticon *(28)* A wood-resin based shell material.

Action 1. *(50)* Describes the feel and sound of a bass drum pedal. 2. Another term for snare strainer. See: *Snare strainer.*

Base plate *(51)* Extra, stabilizing plate for bass drum and hi-hat pedals.

Bass drum *(3–4, 5–6, 37–40)* The largest drum in a kit, played with a pedal.

Bass drum pedal *(3–4, 48–53)* The pedal used to play the bass drum. *Double pedals* or *twin pedals* allow you to use two feet to play one drum, removing the need for a second bass drum.

Batter head See: *Heads.*

Bead See: *Tip.*

Bearing edge *(29–30)* The edge of a drum's shell, which 'bears' the head.

Beater *(52)* The removable part of a bass drum pedal that actually beats the drum.

Bell See: *Cup.*

Boom stand *(9, 56–58)* A cymbal stand with an extra arm that can be set up in almost any position.

Bracket *(5)* The arms of a tom holder and the legs of a floor tom are held in place with brackets.

Brushes *(69–70)* An alternative to sticks, brushes have steel or nylon strands with which you hit or 'stroke' drums and cymbals. Also known as *wire brushes*.

Chinese cymbal *(76–77)* A cymbal with an up-turned edge. As well as authentic Chinese cymbals, many Western variations are available.

Clutch *(54, 97)* The clamp that secures the top hi-hat cymbal to the pull rod.

Concert toms *(47)* Single-headed toms. Also known as *melodic toms*.

Counter hoop See: *Hoop*.

Crash, crash cymbal *(3–4, 8–9, 74, 75–76)* Fast-speaking cymbal, mainly used for accenting and adding colour.

Cup *(9, 74, 76)* The 'bulge' in the middle of a cymbal, also known as the *bell*, often used for penetrating ride patterns in Latin rhythms.

Cymbals *(22–23, 71–79)* Deceptively simple-looking discs of metal, usually bronze. Hundreds of sizes, shapes, types and gauges are available.

Dampening See: *Muffling*.

Dot *(62)* A circular area (usually made of a thin piece of drum head material) in the middle of a drum head. Dries out the sound and helps prevent denting.

Double pedal See: *Bass drum pedal*.

Double-braced *(56)* Double-braced stands have legs that are made of two metal strips, as opposed to one.

Drop-lock clutch *(54–55)* Type of clutch that allows you to 'drop' the top cymbal onto the bottom cymbal. See also: *Clutch*.

Drum key *(81)* T-shaped tool for tuning drums; also available in speed and ratchet versions.

Drum machine *(18–19, 107)* Electronic timekeeping device, played and programmed using buttons and other controls.

Drum rack *(58–59)* Replaces the bottom sections of cymbal stands, microphone stands and so on. Especially useful for large kits.

Electronic drums *(16, 107)* Pads with built-in electronic sensors that respond to your playing, triggering sounds that are stored in a sound module. These sounds are mostly digitally recorded (samples).

Flesh hoop *(5, 30, 93)* The hoop of a drum head, usually made of aluminium.

Floating heads *(31)* Drums with slightly undersized shells have floating heads.

Floor tom *(3, 7, 40, 42)* Three-legged drum, most popular in 16x16 size.

Flush bracing See: *Lugs.*

Fusion kit *(7, 121)* Fusion is a musical mixture of rock and jazz elements, and it led to the creation of the fusion drum kit, which usually features 10" and 12" rack toms and suspended floor toms.

Hardware *(9–10, 21–22, 48–60)* Stands, pedals, holders, lugs, tension rods, washers, bolts and all other metal items in a drum kit (except cymbals).

Heads *(4, 5, 7–8, 22, 44–45, 47, 61–65, 81, 82)* Drum heads are made of one or two plies of polyester film. The sound is determined by their thickness and various other factors such as additional coatings, dots, fillings, holes and built-in muffling rings. Most drums have two heads: a *top* or *batter* head and a *bottom* or *resonant* head (called *snare-side head* on snare drums, and *front head* on bass drums).

High-tension lugs See: *Lugs.*

Hi-hat *(3–4, 8–10)* Two cymbals of equal size *(74–75, 96–97)* and a stand with a pedal *(53–56)* that operates them. Almost always positioned so as to be playable with the left foot.

Hoop *(5, 32–33, 39, 46)* Drums are tuned by tightening up the hoops which stretch the head over the shell. Also known as counter hoops. See also: *Flesh hoop* and *Triple-flanged hoops.*

Isolated mounting system *(44, 85)* A system introduced by Gary Gauger for isolating drums, especially rack toms, from their mounting hardware, to enhance their sound and resonance.

Key bolts, key rods See: *Tension rods.*

Lathed cymbals *(72, 111)* Most cymbals are lathed.

The lathing knife creates the circular pattern of grooves on the cymbal's surface, which open-up its sound. Unlathed cymbals have a tighter sound.

Left-handed drummers *(10, 98)* Left-handed players have a number of options when it comes to setting-up their kit.

Lug bolts See: *Tension rods.*

Lugs, lug casings *(5, 32, 33–35)* Metal casings which house the lug nuts into which the tension rods of a drum are screwed. Also known as *tension mounts*. If a drum is said to have *flush bracing, long lugs, double lugs* or *high-tension lugs*, this means that each lug receives a tension rod from both the batter and the resonant head. See also: *Nodal points.*

Mallets *(70, 106)* Sticks with large heads that are usually covered with felt (like timpani mallets) or wound with yarn (such as xylophone mallets). If someone 'plays mallets', they play mallet instruments such as the vibraphone, xylophone and marimba.

Melodic toms See: *Concert toms.*

Memory locks *(43)* Metal clamps that help you set up quickly. Originally a trade name. Other names include *key locks* and *stop locks.*

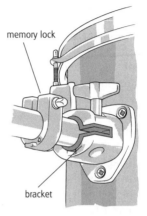

memory lock

bracket

A memory lock on a tom holder

Metronome *(18–19)* Device that clicks or beeps to help you keep a steady tempo.

Muffling *(90–94)* There are many different ways to muffle or dampen drums, each of which has a different effect on the sound.

Multi-clamp *(59)* Piece of hardware used to clamp holders to stands or racks.

Mylar *(63)* A Dupont trade name for the polyester film from which drum heads are made. Often used as a generic term.

Nodal points Drum shells are said to have nodal

points. These indicate positions at which there is no vibration. It is claimed that mounting lugs and brackets on those spots enhances the drum's resonance, though not all experts agree on this point.

Oil *(64)* Two-ply heads often look as though they have oil between the plies, though in most cases they don't.

O-ring *(63–64, 92–93)* Ring cut out of the film from which heads are made. Popular for muffling snare drums.

Pad *(15–16)* A device to enable quiet practice. The most basic pad is a wooden plank with a piece of rubber on top. See also: *Electronic drums.*

Ported bass drum head *(91)* A bass drum front head with a hole in it.

Power toms *(7, 28, 41–42)* Toms with deep shells. Like power cymbals they're primarily designed for heavy players.

Practice pad See: *Pad.*

Pull rod *(54)* The rod to which you attach your top hi-hat cymbal. It 'pulls' the

top down towards the bottom cymbal.

Rack *(58–59)* See: *Drum rack.*

Rack toms *(7, 40–41)* The smaller toms in a kit, which are mounted either on the bass drum or on a drum rack.

Reinforcement hoops *(30)* Wooden rings around the edges of a drum. They reinforce the shell and also influence the sound.

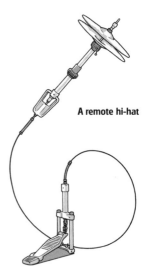

A remote hi-hat

Remote hi-hat *(55)* A hi-hat system with the pedal connected to the section holding the cymbals via a long cable. Often used for a second pair of hi-hat cymbals on the right-hand side of the kit. See also: *X-hat.*

Resonant head See: *Head.*

Ride cymbal *(3–4, 8, 73–74)* A type of cymbal primarily used for time-keeping – you play time, the 'ride', on it. Generally the ride cymbal is the heaviest and largest in a set.

RIMS *(44)* A type of isolated mounting system invented by Gary Gauger. See also: *Isolated mounting system.*

Rivets *(77)* Inserting one or more rivets into a cymbal turns it into a sizzle cymbal.

Seamless Some snare drums and hoops are seamless, meaning they are forced out of a flat metal disc, thus eliminating the need for a welded seam.

Shell *(4, 27–31, 109–110)* The sound chamber of a drum. The shell is the bit that's left if every component (heads, lugs, bracket, etc) is removed from a drum.

Shell kit *(21)* A kit sold without stands or pedals.

Single lugs See: *Lugs.*

Sizzle cymbal *(77)* A cymbal with rivets that produces a 'sizzling' sound.

Snare, snare drum *(3–4, 5, 6–7, 35–37)* One of the two main drums of the drum kit. Both its name and its sound come from the set of snares (wires) which run against its bottom head.

Snare bed *(37)* A snare drum is slightly shallower where the snare strings, or straps, run over its edge. This recess, referred to as the snare bed, helps the snares to lie flat against the snare-head over the entire diameter of the drum.

Snare strainer *(6, 36–37)* A device that allows you to adjust the tension of the snares and to disengage them ('turn them off'). Other names include *snare mechanism, throw-off* and *action.*

Snare-side head *(37, 63, 87–88)* The bottom head of a snare drum, which is very thin.

Snares *(36, 87–88, 89)* The spiralled wires which run across the bottom head of a snare drum. There are usually about twenty of them.

Spring tension *(10, 49, 50, 53–54)* Determines how heavy or light a pedal feels.

Adjustable on all bass drum pedals and most hi-hat pedals.

Square drum sizes *(41, 42)* Drums whose depth equals their diameter (such as 12x12).

Stands *(3–4, 9–10, 56–58)* Pieces of hardware for holding toms, cymbals, snare drums or other pieces of equipment.

Stool *(59–60)* A drummer's seat. The term *throne* is also used.

Suspended cymbal *(106)* The classical music term for a cymbal on a stand.

Symmetrical drum sizes See: *Square drum sizes.*

Tension mounts See: *Lugs.*

Tension rods, tension screws, tension bolts *(5, 33–34, 38–39)* The special metal rods that are used to alter the tension in the head. They're also known as key rods, lug bolts and key bolts.

Throne See: *Stool.*

Throw-off See: *Snare strainer.*

Tilter *(9–10, 96–97)* The

section of a stand that enables part of it to tilt. You'll find a tilter on all cymbal stands, snare drum stands and tom arms. *Ratchet tilters* or *gear tilters* use two sets of interlocking teeth; toothless tilters allow for finer adjustment. Hi-hat stands have a different type of tilter – a screw that lets you tilt the bottom cymbal.

Tip *(67)* The end of a drumstick; also called the *bead*. Most sticks have wooden tips, but others have nylon ones, which sound brighter, especially on cymbals. Many shapes and sizes of tip are available.

Tom holder *(42–44)* Mount for rack toms.

Toms, tom toms *(7, 40–42)* The 'other' drums in a kit besides the snare drum and bass drum. May either be mounted (rack toms) or on legs (floor toms).

Trigger pad A drum pad with built-in electronic sensors that recognizes when it's hit and triggers a sound module. See also: *Electronic drums* and *Pad.*

Triple-flanged hoops Pressed hoops usually have

three flanges (angled surfaces). The upper one, which was added last, protects your sticks from the biting effect of rimshots.

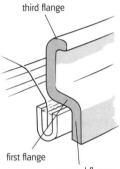

third flange

first flange

second flange

Tuning *(80–90)* Some say you can't really 'tune' a drum, as it doesn't have a definite pitch. However, tuning is the standard term to describe adjusting the tension of a head of a drum to change its sound.

Twin pedal See: *Bass drum pedal.*

Wire brushes See: *Brushes.*

X-hat *(55)* A stand for an extra pair of hi-hat cymbals (originally a trade name). See also: *Remote hi-hat.*

WANT TO KNOW MORE?

This book gives you all the basics you need for buying, maintaining, tuning and using drums, drum heads, cymbals and sticks. If you want to know more, there are lots of magazines, books and Web sites you could turn to.

MAGAZINES

There are a number of drummers' magazines that feature interviews, product reviews and other articles. You won't find all of the magazines in the following list at your local newsagent, but check the Web sites for subscription information.

- *Rhythm* (UK) No Web site at present; phone 01225 442244
- *Modern Drummer* (US) www.moderndrummer.com
- *Drum!* (US) www.drumlink.com
- *Stick It* (US) www.stickitonline.com
- *Not So Modern Drummer* (US; dedicated to vintage drums) www.notsomoderndrummer.com
- *Percussive Notes* (US; published by the Percussive Arts Society) www.pas.org
- *Latin Percussionist* (US) www.latinpercussion.com

BOOKS

Most books on drums deal largely with the history of the instrument, but some titles also cover modern drums. The following list contains examples of both.

- *The Cymbal Book*, by Hugo Pinksterboer (Hal Leonard, USA, 1993; 212 pages; ISBN 07 935 1920 9).
- *The Drum Book, A History of the Rock Drum Kit*, by Geoff

Nichols (Balafon, England, 1997; 112 pages; ISBN 1 871 547 25 3).

- *The Drummer's Almanac*, by Jon Cohan (Hal Leonard, USA, 1998; 80 pages; ISBN 07 9356 696 7).
- *The Drummer's Studio Survival Guide*, by Mark Huntley Parsons (Modern Drummer Publications, USA, 1996; 94 pages; ISBN 7935 7222 3).
- *The Great American Drums and the Companies that Made Them*, 1920–1969, by Harry Cangany (Hal Leonard, USA, 1996; 72 pages; ISBN 07 9356 356 9).
- *Gretsch Drums – The Legacy of that Great Gretsch Sound*, by Chet Falzerano (Centerstream, USA, 1996; 144 pages; ISBN 09 3175 998 6).
- *Guide to Vintage Drums*, by John Aldridge (Centerstream, USA, 1996; 174 pages; ISBN 09 3175 979 X).
- *History of Leedy Drum Co.: The World's Largest Drum Co.*, by Rob Cook (Centerstream, USA, 1996; 178 pages; ISBN 09 3175 974 9).
- *Star Sets: Drum Kits of the Great Drummers*, by Jon Cohan (Hal Leonard, USA, 1995; 160 pages; ISBN 07 9353 489 5).

INTERNET

The Internet is an excellent source of information on both equipment and drummers. Links to lots of drum-related sites can be found at sites like www.drums.com, www.drums.about.com, www.drumweb.com, www.cyberdrum.com and www.drumline.com.

ESSENTIAL DATA

In the event of your equipment being stolen or lost, or even if you just decide to sell it, it's useful to have all the relevant information, such as serial numbers and original prices, to hand. Here are two pages to make these notes.

INSURANCE

Insurance company:

Phone: Fax:

Broker:

Phone: Fax:

Policy no.:

Premium:

DRUM KIT

Make and series:

Color:

Price:

Date of purchase:

Place of purchase:

Phone: Fax:

DRUMS

Sizes, serial numbers, and other relevant data per drum.

1

2

3

4

5

6

7

8

9

10

CYMBALS

Brand name, series, size, date of purchase, price, serial number, and/or other data per cymbal. Most cymbals come without a serial number; if there is one you'll find it on the inside of the cup.

1 _____
2 _____
3 _____
4 _____
5 _____
6 _____
7 _____
8 _____
9 _____
10 _____

ACCESSORIES AND OTHER INSTRUMENTS

1 _____
2 _____
3 _____
4 _____
5 _____
6 _____
7 _____
8 _____

ADDITIONAL NOTES

....
....
....
....
....
....
....
....
....
....
....
....

ADDITIONAL NOTES